# How to Succeed in Your Work

## CONTENTS

# 1. How to Succeed in Your Work

There are many aspects to following a successful career. They are mostly derived from two characteristics of personality: ability and application. A person with much ability has an easier time than another who is less able but the individual with less ability can also succeed through greater application.

**Ability** covers a person's capacity to solve problems by logical means. This has been called intelligence. However, just being clever is not sufficient to ensure career success. Intelligence must be balanced with personality: how a person behaves in a particular situation – whether a leader or a follower, diplomatic or forthright, assertive or sociable, formal or relaxed, decisive or hesitant. All of these characteristics will contribute to the ease with which a person can fit into an organisation.

**Application** is related to how hard a person tries. Physical fitness can be defined in terms of strength, stamina, suppleness, skill and psychological drive or determination. So it is with fitness to succeed in employment. The psychological drive is the will to succeed. Skill comes from knowing the rules and practising them to a level of competence. Suppleness is the flexibility to survive in changing situations. Stamina means perseverance through the tough times, when dealing with difficult situations or temperamental colleagues. Strength is acquired by training and it does not come easily. Application means applying all of these characteristics in the context of employment.

This collection of work-connected articles covers a wide range of the tools necessary to get employment, to do a good job and to progress. As a tradesperson needs first to know his tools and then to practice with them, so administrative skills are not gained in a moment. *"I hear and I forget. I see and I remember. I do and I understand"*. So this compendium contains some tools. They are not to be learned parrot-fashion, but applied thoughtfully and critically because circumstances change and not every tool can be used in the same way in every situation.

These guidelines are intended to help you and your colleagues avoid some pitfalls and to be able to do better what you may already do well.

# 2. How to Write Your Résumé (Curriculum Vitae)

The selector or human resource officer reviewing your application for a post or promotion
will be looking for three things – 'CAN, WILL, and FIT'     **A)  CAN** this person do the job?

    **B)  WILL** this person accept the job if offered? (If the candidate can do the work too easily
      without being challenged, interest may not be sustained and the candidate may leave
      through boredom)

    **C)**  Will the candidate **FIT** the ethos of the organisation and the team?


Here are some general guidelines which will help the construction of your *curriculum vitae* (CV)
or résumé. These are:

1. Keep a full CV in which you record all the details of your professional life. This is
   increasingly important as you get older and your CV longer. From this you can select
   material specifically for answering a job advertisement. (You can find a choice of
   suggested formats and headings in MS Publisher/File/New/Publications for
   Print/Résumé)
2. Start with your personal details and contact information. If  you add a photograph,
   make sure it is appropriate. And look friendly; smile!
3. Include your mission statement – where you want to be in 5 years time
4. Avoid using the personal pronoun 'I'
5. Always be truthful. Experienced interviewers are skilful in checking consistency
6. Use bullet points rather than full text
7. List work experience from the latest backwards
8. Leave some white space to allow the reader to add comments: do not feel obliged to
   fill all the space
9. Do not miss out any time: missed periods raise suspicion
10. Include evaluative statements in several instances but always in a positive way e.g.
    "This project was not completed as funding was withdrawn". "Reports were always
    presented on time which led to increased productivity". (This is a better approach than
    simply listing experiences without indicating their success or otherwise). "Am currently
    studying" is better than stating "Little knowledge of Runyankore", especially if
    Runyankore language is requested
11. Use the 'footer' for page number, date and computer location of document
12. Indicate religious, political activities, sports and leisure pursuits. These may form a link
    with the interviewer who shares your hobbies/beliefs. While you are not legally obliged
    to give this information, some of the associated skills may be transferable. Or they can
    exclude you from a post in which you may be unhappy through conflict of personal
    interests. If you include "Reading", then add an extension e.g. "Reading Chinese
    poetry"
13. Give referees and their contact details but add a note asking for them not to be
    contacted without prior permission. (Your choice of referees tells much about your
    associates and may be particularly significant for educational posts.) This will allow you
    to contact them first to update them with your latest CV and a copy of the job
    description so the referees write references appropriate for the post
14. Keep to three pages (two to four maximum) (difficult for older people with longer
    experiences!). Your CV should pass the '20 seconds' test. Remember that the person
    reading it may have hundreds more on the desk to be scrutinised. Ending your CV with
    a statement like, "I certify that this document is a true record of my life activities and
    contains the truth, the whole truth and nothing but the truth" is generally a waste of
    space
15. Spell and grammar check it thoroughly (making sure you use the correct form of English

i.e. USA or UK etc if that is the language being used). Take the opportunity to remove repetitious and unnecessary words

16.     Ask somebody else to read it through because your 'spell checker' will not pick up an inappropriate word if spelled correctly e.g. 'there' instead of 'their'

17.     Keep your CV updated. Important details, such as dates or publication details, are easily forgotten with the passing of time.

Now put yourself in the position of a Head of Human Resources. What CV improvements might you suggest to Natalie and Gloria? Then write your own CV.

## *Natalie Craigen*

*345 Huan Dao Dong Road*
*Mei Jiang Nan Residence Zone*
*Tianjin*
*China.*

*Phone : +86 (0)2225 478596.  Email : NatalieCr@hotmail.com*


### *PRIMARY SCHOOL TEACHER*

Professional experience gained within varied practical and development roles, mainly within Modern Sport. (games, gymnastics, athletics, swimming, P.E., outdoor education). Believing a mature, constructive and eclectic teaching approach and effective working relationships between staff, students and parents are crucial to a responsive student attitude, a successful learning environment and meeting the needs of children and school mandates. Now looking to make a continued significant contribution for a school in an international setting, preferably as a Classroom Teacher, a Specialist Primary P.E. Teacher, Key Stage Co-ordinator or a position of similar responsibility.

## AREAS OF EXPERTISE

- Sports /P.E. Development
- Planning in compliance with N.C.
- Communication in early years
- Organising programmes
- Differentiating learning activities
- Policy and plan construction

- Primary liaison work
- Curriculum co-ordination
- Extra curricular teams
- Organising house events
- Diversity (Equal Ops.)
- Pastoral care

- Outdoor education
- Staff mentoring
- Computer literacy
- Organising productions
- Teamwork
- Writing plans / reports

## PROFESSIONAL DEVELOPMENT

| | | |
|---|---|---|
| **Bachelor of Education** | Junior Primary / Junior (University of South Australia, Majoring in Psychology and Physical Education). | **1996 - 00** |
| **Certificate** | Psychology and Child Development (Open Learning) | **1995** |

**Other certifications** / professional training courses have supplemented my extensive hands-on experience: First Aid, Sports Medicine, Surf Survival, Fitness Leadership, Swimming Instructor (AUSWIM), Mandatory Notification Training, Aerobics Instructor, Taekwondo Instructor (Black belt), Numeracy strategy, Literacy insets including ESL children in literacy, KS2 Grammar for writing, Computer literacy (ICT).

## PROFESSIONAL EXPERIENCE AND SIGNIFICANT ACHIEVEMENTS

### CLASS TEACHER (YEAR 5)                                 *Oct 03 - Present*
*Rego International School, Tianjin China  (http://www.regoschool.org)*

Teacher of all subjects within the Primary Curriculum, including maths, design and technology games, gymnastics, athletics, swimming and Physical Education as well as National Numeracy and Literacy strategies. Supervising one Classroom Assistant, organising events, PTA evenings and pastoral care.
- Gained experience of teaching children with English as a second language.
- Designed visual and interactive lessons and organised English language sleepovers mainly for the 90% of the students that are Korean, (speaking little or no English).
- Encouraged parents to be actively involved in many areas of school life whilst developing close working relationships an active PTA and an open door policy.
- Advised and supported staff on planning, assessment and resources, including lesson modelling.
- Organised, lunchtime and after school clubs,  sponsored events and speak only English days.
- Organised the opening ceremony that involved a major performance including dance, song and music.
- Assisted in overseeing S.A.T. programme including moderation and agreement trailing.
- Introduced year-by-year programme of Grammar and Punctuation work.
- Planned and developed assessment procedures with P.E. and implemented IT within this process.
- Restructured P.E. programme and delivered new and successful P.E. course.
- Ran the team sports' club (many Regional Leagues).
- Met all increasing intake demands.
- Identified gaps and drew up schemes and policies to ensure a broader curriculum is covered.

---

**TUMUSHABE GLORIA MPAKA**          *CURRICULUM VITAE*  **January 2008**

**Biographic Information**

| | |
|---|---|
| **Date of birth** | 4 May 1979 |
| **Home district** | Rukungiri |
| **Nationality** | Ugandan |
| **Civil status** | Single |
| **Address** | Temporarily residing in Mbarara Town but prepared to move anywhere |
| **Telephone** | +256 (0) 772578105 |

## 1. Career Aims

- To achieve my potential through a satisfying professional career in a way that is of value to the community by providing services and support to those that need it

- To use my skills and experience for the benefit of the organisation and the people it serves

- To develop further my knowledge and competencies through this work

## 2. Education

| | |
|---|---|
| 2000 – 2002 | YMCA, Mbarara (part-time). Diploma in Catering and Hotel Management awarded (placed in top third) |
| 1995 – 1996 | Kampala Students' Centre. U.A.C.E. Passed History, Economics, Divinity and General Paper |
| 1990 – 1993 | Kyamakanda Secondary School. U.C.E. Passed in nine subjects |
| 1982 – 1988 | Kihumuro Primary School. P.L.E. All examinations passed |

## 3. Languages

English - fluent written and spoken
Runyankole    - excellent
Luganda       - fluent written and spoken

## 4. Key Skills

Management in hotel and catering
Enjoy and able to deal with different types of people
Computing and communication skills
Accounting

## 5. Personality Summary

Ready to face challenges
Honesty and integrity
Able to plan and be advised
Flexible: ready to work either as an individual or in a team
Sharing knowledge and experiences with others
Effective communication skills with people at all levels
Committed and stable
Enthusiastic and a quick learner.

## 6. Other Information

Head girl in Secondary School
Chairperson of School Music, Dance and Drama
Active in netball and other sports when time allows

Reading novels and current media
Desire to learn more, attend workshops, and enjoy adventuring and travel

## 8. Professional Experience

| Date from – to | **July 2006 – present** |
|---|---|
| *Company* | Hotel Classic Ltd<br>Mbarara |
| *Position* | Restaurant Supervisor |
| *Description* | Responsible for staff management and customer service<br>Supervision of services and customer care<br>Reporting to General Manager. |

| Date from – to | **April 2000-2003** |
|---|---|
| *Company* | Hotel Classic Ltd<br>Mbarara |
| *Position* | Cashier |
| *Description* | Maintaining correct accounts of all customer transactions. This involved working long hours to complete the task, and handling demanding customers with diplomacy<br><br>Supervision of other staff handling money<br>Responsible to General Manager for all aspects of accounting |

(1989 and 1994 were periods awaiting commencement of further studies. 1997-1999 was occupied with domestic responsibilities at home.)

## 9. Referees. (Please do not contact without my prior permission)

1. Mr Mugarura Benon
   General Manager
   Hotel Classic
   PO Box 1162
   Mbarara

2. Mr Emeroit Johns
   General Manager
   Savana Hotel
   Tel.    0652 423999

3. The Principal
   YMCA
   Mbarara
   PO Box 259 Tel.
           0452
   507730

# 3. How to Apply for a Post

Consider two letters of application.

Dear Sir/Madom

APLICATION FOR THE POST OF ............................................

I wish to apply for the post of ..........................

I assure you that if I appointed I will work to the best of my abilities and for the betterment of your organisation.

Please find enclosed a capy of my resume.

Thank you.

Yours faithfully,

In the first:

- it is brief and easily read
- but the letter is addressed impersonally and contains spelling mistakes. There is wasteful repetition of the post title
- there is no indication of where the advert was seen, which does not help the employer to know which of several publications are the most useful for future post advertisements
- there is no information that will entice the reader to continue reading the CV
- there is no indication, other than the promise of loyalty, of anything that the candidate can add to the required qualities
- the font type may be seen as frivolous and not business-like

In the second:

- the letter is addressed to a named person
- more space is taken up than in the first but it carries much more information and is still contained on one side of A4 paper

-   the source of the advertisement is given
-   the requirements are related to the qualities and experiences of the candidate
-   where the candidate does not have requirements (e.g. experience of Africa) other experiences are offered that could be transferable e.g. worked in Asia. The candidate does not have an education degree but does have ten years experience in teaching
-   other skills are offered which are not demanded by the post but which could well be important to the employer
-   the confident ending shows the candidate is keen
-   in a few seconds the reader has learned enough of the applicant to want to see the CV

Dear Ms Bluebell

I wish to apply for the post of **Assistant Project Officer – African Refugee Children** as described in "Refugees Records" (27.06.2011).

I have experience of working in the conflict areas of Asia, of working with children and young people, interviewing, training, negotiating with the local and other authorities, and I am committed to assisting the peace process in 2011 to become sustainable.

| You require | My experience |
| --- | --- |
| A degree in Social Work, Education, or Psychology | In-service training in Education, BSc Chemistry (with Physiology), MSc Pharmacology, More than ten years teaching experience. |
| Training experience | Extensive experience in training, and training of trainers for international, national and local organisations |
| Computer literacy | Recent update in MS Office Professional courses obtaining Merit in MS Word |
| Ability to work in a cross-cultural environment | In addition to working in Israel, have worked in Asia with Muslim, Hindu and Christian colleagues. |
| Psychosocial programmes dealing with children | Worked with children's camps in the UK and with street children in Brazil. |

In further support of my application I have excellent writing skills, strong organisation and communication abilities. I can work independently (in isolation if necessary) and expect to deliver a finished product on time.

 My *curriculum vitae* and contact details of three referees are attached and I look forward with optimism to hearing from you.


Yours sincerely




Angola Julian BSc MSc
Deputy Head Teacher, Krachi Secondary School

When you send an application for a post put yourself in the position of the selection personnel. They are busy people who may be dealing with several vacancies and several hundred applications at the same time. If there is only one opening, it is of little comfort to know that you were the second or third choice. Your application has to stand out among the others. What devices are available for achieving this? Here are some ideas for you to consider: not all are appropriate in all situations.

1. Print your CV on lightly tinted paper or in a different font colour: dark blue is good: it must be suitable for photocopying.
2. Choose the font type carefully and do not change this in the rest of the document
3. Address your application to a named person. You may have to telephone the company to obtain the details
4. Avoid sending your application by email. If this has to be done, back it up with a hard copy or a fax. Emails can easily be ignored and they do not carry the compulsion of attention demanded by a hard copy
5. Research the organisation thoroughly and read the advertisement/job description carefully so you supply the information that is required for the post. Show that you will 'fit' into the organisation if offered the position. Build their key words into your application
6. Indicate that you have more to offer than is being requested
7. Knock on doors! This can be useful if you are exploring opportunities where vacancies have not been advertised. Ask if somebody in the organisation could spare you time to explain more about their activities (having read brochures or web site information). Some have struck lucky and landed a post that was about to be advertised.
8. Offer to work for nothing in order to gain experience. Many have been given this opportunity and later been offered a permanent appointment having proved their worth
9. Include short examples of your work e.g. a report, publication or article/brochure that you have prepared.

# <u>4. How to Groom for an Interview</u>

You have been invited to attend an interview for a new job or promotion! What can you expect? Almost certainly you have been interviewed before but this one might be different. Interviewers can adopt one or more of several styles and you may have to confront different interviewing groups who are looking for different information. The interview process could be brief, or spread over several days. You may be interviewed at the head office of the organisation in your country, and additionally by field staff from the District where you hope to be destined. If you live far away you may be offered a telephone interview, or increasingly a video interview.

Interview methods and approaches include:
1. One-to-one. This may be formally across the desk of an office, or relaxed in a café or restaurant
2. Group interview. Panel members take turns to ask questions covering different aspects of the work
3. Stress interviews. Stories are told of coffee being 'accidentally' spilled on candidates to measure reactions to stress. More likely are group games or simulations under time pressure in the presence of a management psychologist who records your leadership/team qualities, response to pressure etc
4. Scenarios. You may be given a humanitarian scenario and asked to write an essay on "How you would deal with it"
5. Psychometric tests. These are intended to measure your aptitudes and qualities or personality characteristics. Many can be freely downloaded from internet for practice (see section 12)
6. Presentations. You can be asked to come prepared with a presentation on a given topic, or asked to prepare one during the interview period
7. In-tray exercise. A pile of documents needs your responses. Make sure you read all the documents before responding to any of them as some lower in the pile may modify or cancel actions suggested by those higher up!
8. Candidate groups. Generally you will not meet other applicants for a single post to prevent experience swapping. However, if several candidates are needed to form a team, you may be interviewed with others and subjected to group activities

The success of an interview depends upon the match between you and the interviewers. The outcome is influenced by some unknowns (the psychology of the people and the 'chemistry' between them), luck (common interests), and known factors (the organisation ethos and needs, and your experience and qualifications). So, control the aspects within your power.

1. Investigate the organisation's culture, programmes, and finances. But resist the temptation to show off what you've researched unless you have a question directly related to your career

2.  Arrive before time, visit the toilet and introduce yourself with a firm handshake. Look as if you already belong. Learn the dress code and err on the side of conservatism (a prior visit could establish this)
3.  Listen carefully to the questions and take charge of the interview! The most successful interviews feel like friendly conversations. When your interviewer has an agenda (such as the infamous "stress interview") stay relaxed. Think of it as playing a game
4.  Assume everyone you meet will provide feedback to the decision-maker. Some companies hand out comment forms to security guards, receptionists, and potential peers who take you to lunch
5.  Communicate interest and enthusiasm by use of body language, even if you're not sure you're ready to commit to the job. You'll rarely have all the facts until you're looking at an offer
6.  Know your résumé and be able to summarise your achievements. Add value judgements
7.  Have a clear reason for change. E.g. "I have been in my current company for X years and want to become a manager" i.e. a professional reason. NOT "I can't get along with my boss" (you may not get on with next one!) You may wish to extend your budget responsibilities, man management, or general responsibilities. But link your information to the actual job
8.  Try to avoid saying "No" as an answer. "Are you fluent in Luganda?" could be a question. Perhaps not, but you could reply, "I fully appreciate the need to have a national language in addition to my Swahili when working with a national team. My Runyankore is good. I learned some Luganda at school and am working hard to become more fluent"
9.  Be prepared for surprise questions unrelated to the previous one e.g. what is the most passionate article you read recently? This checks if you can think on your feet
10. Linguistically use plural forms – "If WE are working together on this project………" This helps the 'Can Will Fit' syndrome
11. When could you start? Do not give away too much. "I can probably start two weeks/one month from the offer"
12. Never abandon an interview part way through. Finish it well – you may meet the interviewer in another situation!
13. Have some questions to ask – the next step, computer/internet availability, starting date, opportunities to travel to other projects, potential for advancement/permanency, etc. Tailor the questions to the level of the interviewer. Don't ask the Vice President about vegetarian food in the restaurant. Sales – "What is the business plan, areas of greatest growth, what is your biggest problem right now? Why did you join the organisation? What has your career path been since you joined?" Thank the interviewers at the end

To be sure that you can make the change into a higher post, some interviewers may ask harder questions:

**What Are Your Weaknesses?**
This is the most dreaded question of all. Minimise your weakness and emphasise your strengths. Stay away from personal qualities and concentrate on professional traits: "I

am always working on improving my communication skills to be a more effective presenter."

## Why Should We Hire You?
 "With five years' experience working in the financial industry and my proven record of saving the company money, I could make a big difference in your organisation. I'm confident I would be a great addition to your team"

## Why Do You Want to Work Here?
The interviewer is listening for an answer that indicates you've given this some thought and are not sending out CVs just because there is an opening. For example, "I've selected key organisations whose mission statements are in line with my values, where I know I could be excited about the work, and this organisation is high on my list of choices"

## When Were You Most Satisfied in Your Job?
The interviewer wants to know what motivates you. If you can relate an example of a job or project when you were excited, the interviewer will get an idea of your preferences. "I was very satisfied in my last job, because I worked directly with the customers and their problems; that is an important part of the job for me and I can relate it to social work"

## What Can You Do for Us That Other Candidates Can't?
What makes you unique? This will take an assessment of your experiences, skills and traits. Summarise concisely: "I have a unique combination of strong technical skills, and the ability to build strong personal relationships especially in cross-cultural situations"

## What Are Three Positive Things Your Last Boss Would Say About You?
It's time to pull out your old performance appraisals and boss's quotes. This is a fine way to brag about yourself through someone else's words: "My boss has told me that I am the best engineer he has ever had. He knows he can rely on me, and he likes my sense of humour"

## If You Were an Animal, Which One Would You Want to Be?
Interviewers use this type of psychological question to see if you can think quickly. If you answer "a rabbit," you will make a soft, passive impression. If you answer "a lion," you will be seen as aggressive. What type of personality would it take to get the job done? What impression do you want to make?

Moving from one post to another with more responsibility could transport you into a whole new world of management, financial control, report and proposal writing, or dealing with refugees, conflict and human rights abuses. Your preparation may need to include reading about any of these issues, or at least discussing them with someone who already has those responsibilities. Management needs to be learned: it is not a function that just comes automatically, so prepare well.

# <u>5. How to Make Your Mission Statements</u>

**6.1 Writing Two Mission Statements**

Now you are established in your new employment and perhaps in a new location that you may not have visited before. Your motivation is high and you want to give all you can while gaining as much as possible during the course of your contract. A job description has been provided but it may have changed during the several months between the time it was written and your arrival. Your briefing and induction are behind you. Sometimes your employer will be looking to you for ideas about how you will proceed.

While on contract it is good to have two mission statements. One is your professional mission and the other is your personal one.

**6.2 A professional mission statement**

The success of your professional vocation will depend upon your ability and application to your work, but it will also be influenced strongly by your colleagues, the line manager, the office conditions, bureaucratic procedures, available resources and external domestic, cultural and political conditions. In the worst situation, you may not be concerned with succeeding in your work, only surviving it! In other words, your mission in this post is not totally under your control. However, draft a professional mission statement and share it with your boss or line manager.

**Professional Mission Statement for Jo Soper - 01.01.2011.**

**Manager, Child Soldier Rehabilitation Centre**

**Mission**

To facilitate the rehabilitation and reintegration of child soldiers with their community and families

**Aims**

1. To manage the rehabilitation centre
2. To provide training for staff
3. To maintain an appropriate environment for the rehabilitation of released child soldiers
4. To ensure security arrangements for the buildings and occupants

**Objectives**

1. Participate in weekly meetings with staff
2. Provide technical advice to staff
3. Develop modalities of working processes and protocols
4. Ensure all children are interviewed on entry
5. Oversee national staff for interviewing, psychosocial provision, reporting and documentation
6. Update and maintain a highly secure database of children
7. Represent organisation at meetings with other agencies involved in the centre
8. Liaise with social work teams and other agencies involved in the release and reintegration of under-age recruits (SCF, UNDP)
9. Undertake any other work reasonably requested by Supervisor
10. Gain knowledge necessary for the above responsibilities

**Tasks**

1. Hold weekly staff meetings
2. Attend Friday Planning meeting in Zone Office on alternate weeks
3. Prepare for Social Work Training Workshop 15-20 December
4. Visit neighbouring Rehab Centre
5. Write Fire Precaution Guidelines
6. Create Accident Report Form
7. Train staff in Fire Precautions and hold fire drill
8. Train all staff in security using the security CD
9. Draft security and emergency procedures
10. Complete Monthly Report Form for HQ

A more advanced way of setting out your mission is to tabulate it in the form of a logical framework analysis or log frame. Several variations exist and a clear description of this tool is to be found under Proposal Writing in www.ausaid.gov.au.

Simply, a log frame extends the format on the previous page by tabulating alongside each objective the expected outcome, and the actual task. The logic becomes evident if you start looking at the Action which will result in the Outcome, and so on. However, the table starts to become complex as each objective may have more than one outcome. You can be helped by numbering each box as the sections and subsections of this booklet have been numbered.

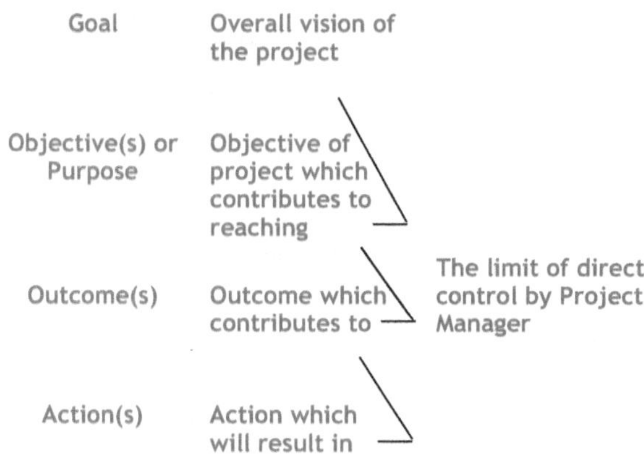


Additional columns can be added for 'Indicators of Achievement', 'Means of Verification' and 'Risks and Assumptions.

Writing a full log frame requires some practice and dedication so you might opt for a shorter version like the one above although it is improved by including indicators of achievement thus allowing you to monitor your progress. Those of you who will need to write project or funding proposals should endeavour to master the more elaborate versions of log frames as many donors insist on their inclusion in a concept paper or proposal document.

## 6.3 A personal mission statement.

While you are in this new situation, perhaps for a year or more, you want to gain as much as you can from the experience. You must build some leisure time into your programme especially if you are inclined to be workaholic. So write a simple personal mission statement which you can share with your family or friends and indulge yourself with hobby time or a new activity. This will be almost entirely under your control, so if it fails – that will be your fault!

| | |
|---|---|
| **Personal Mission while in Uganda 2011-2012** | |
| Mission | -    to gain an overview of Ugandan wildlife |
| Aim | -    to visit national parks and Victoria Falls |
| Objectives | -    walk at least one hour 3X/week for fitness |
| -    obtain Field Guide to Birds of Uganda | |
| -    maintain log of birds visiting garden | |
| -    visit mountain gorilla sanctuary etc, etc | |

## 6.4 Planning Your Work Strategy

Work plans are only useful guides if related to a time scale. Short-term or annual contract work can be set out in the form of a bar chart. This is a useful way of adjusting work loads and travel plans to fit in with climatic conditions such as the flood season, and public holidays (which may differ from those in your home country).

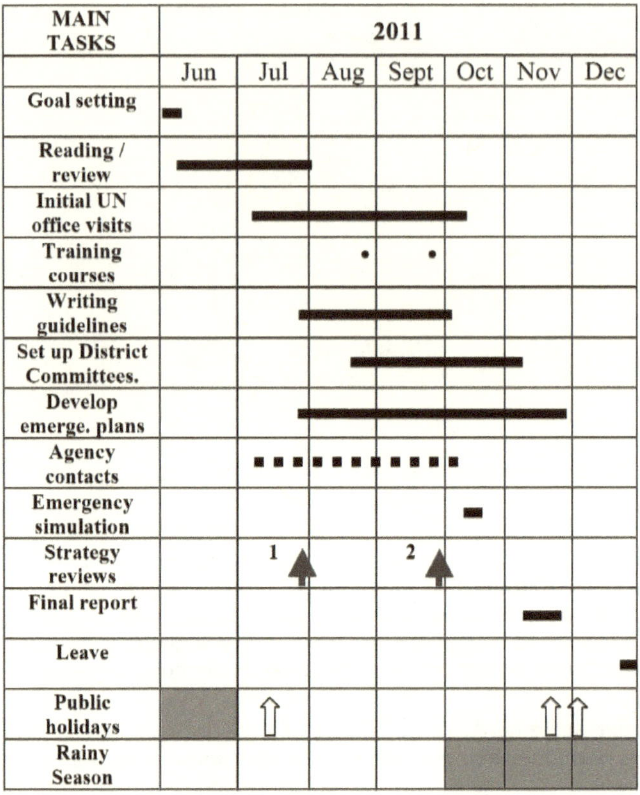

| MAIN TASKS | 2011 | | | | | | |
|---|---|---|---|---|---|---|---|
| | Jun | Jul | Aug | Sept | Oct | Nov | Dec |
| Goal setting | ▬ | | | | | | |
| Reading / review | ▬▬▬▬ | ▬ | | | | | |
| Initial UN office visits | | ▬▬▬ | ▬▬▬ | ▬▬ | | | |
| Training courses | | | ● | ● | | | |
| Writing guidelines | | | ▬▬ | ▬▬ | | | |
| Set up District Committees. | | | | ▬▬▬ | ▬▬ | | |
| Develop emerge. plans | | | ▬▬▬ | ▬▬▬ | ▬▬ | | |
| Agency contacts | | ▪ ▪ ▪ ▪ | ▪ ▪ ▪ | ▪ ▪ ▪ | ▪ | | |
| Emergency simulation | | | | | ▬ | | |
| Strategy reviews | | 1 ⬆ | | 2 ⬆ | | | |
| Final report | | | | | | ▬ | |
| Leave | | | | | | | ▬ |
| Public holidays | �®▬ | ⇧ | | | | ⇧ ⇧ | |
| Rainy Season | | | | | ▒ | ▒ | ▒ |

This chart can be attached to your mission statement.

# 6. How to Appraise Your Work Progress

Many organisations will have trial periods, and appraisal systems which may be quarterly, annual or term: it is common for a final review meeting to be held between employee and employer. This may be formal, informal or conducted through completion of appraisal forms. However, the smart employee will want to be aware of progress during the contract so that adjustments can be made if necessary. There are several ways of achieving this.

One approach is to set out the original objectives in a monthly tabular form and to give yourself a mark (perhaps on a scale of 1-5 or 1-10) for each objective. This will focus your attention on each of the job areas you are addressing. An extended version of this method is to photocopy the table and give it to two or three trusted colleagues who might be familiar with your work, and ask them to assess your activities. Then their assessments can be compared with your self-assessment. Differences can be discussed. The exercise can be extended to the appraisal of your colleagues and repeated for them. You can add notes of explanation and repeat the exercise on a monthly basis.

---

**First Monthly Review for J.S. - 30.09.2011**

1. **Overview**

   The first Strategy document (08.06.2011) remains essentially unchanged. The time scale of activities has been elaborated (appendix 1) and summary notes on each section are provided. No changes have been made to the Mission, Aims, Objectives, Activities, Potential Partners, and Log Frame.

2. **Goal Setting**

   The following activities are all directed towards achieving the goal.

3. **Reading / Review**

   Major UNHCR and other UN publications have been read. "Refugees" and other journals are scanned or read depending on interest. One paper (The Global Disaster Situation) has been written for the National Disaster Management Centre. Another (Village Life with Dignity for the Displaced) has been drafted for publication.

   **Progress 6/10**

4. **Field Office Visits**

   Discussions for briefing and EP working sessions have been held with colleagues, Jaffna (one visit and another planned), Trincomalee (two visits) and Vavuniya (three visits). Visits to Mannar and the uncleared Vanni (Maddhu and Mallavi) have not been possible although discussions have been held with colleagues from the area. Initial resistance......etc the development of emergency preparedness is being overcome, but it remains a problem. Discussions with JD and UNICEF are helping to resolve this difficulty.

   **Progress 5/10**

5. **Training Courses**

   A series of four workshops is being planned for staff, other agencies, and key partners:

   August 22-30      Regional Emergency Management Training Programme

   October 27-28     Contingency Planning and Practice

   November 14-16  Training Trainers for Contingency Planning

   November 26-30  Emergency Management Training Programme for

   Country

   **Progress 2/10**

---

## 7. How to Manage a Meeting

# CONTENTS

21

# 7.1. PURPOSES OF MEETINGS

## 1.1 Introduction

Meetings are a normal, everyday part of humanitarian life. Many of us have experienced coming away from a meeting with a sense of accomplishment and satisfaction, without necessarily knowing why the meeting was successful. Perhaps all of us at sometime remember leaving a meeting with feelings of anger and frustration, wondering what could have been done to have produced a better outcome.

These guidelines are intended to help relative beginners to meetings management avoid some of the pitfalls, to present some best practices, and to help experienced chairpersons, administrators and recorders of minutes do an even better job. Participants should also be able to gain more from formal meetings, and to help the process towards a successful outcome.

## 1.2 Meeting Purposes

Formal meetings take place when people agree to meet for a specific purpose in a set place at a specific time. Such meetings deal with formal agenda items in a systematic manner. But participants and meeting officials may also have their own hidden agendas, perhaps hoping to take the opportunity to air ideas not necessarily related to the matters intended for discussion. These hidden agendas can be legitimate or illegitimate and chairpersons will need to be aware of these possibilities while attempting to complete the formal agenda on time.

Meetings may be arranged for several reasons of which the following list includes some, but not necessarily all, of the main ones:

- To exchange or discuss ideas
- To inform or raise awareness
- To negotiate positions
- To solve problems
- To cover or review a range of different routine issues
- To plan a future activity
- To welcome and introduce new staff/visitors, build relationships, review progress; discuss budgets, strategies, domestic arrangements, outcomes, and planning, and to finalise decision-making processes

Meetings may range from a small group of staff that meet regularly and frequently, to many hundreds of people attending an annual general meeting for the main purpose of receiving progress reports, and electing officials. Similar guidelines can be applied to both of these situations. However, it is important to determine at the earliest stage of planning, whether a meeting is really necessary at all. Potential costs (money, people's time) may indicate that objectives can be reached adequately by the use of a chat in the corridor, a circulated document or a telephone conference.

Telephone conferencing is becoming increasingly available in many countries. Video conferencing requires a microphone, a digital camera, appropriate software and a fast internet connection. These systems can work well especially with relatively small numbers of people who are geographically widely separated, saving travel time, costs and jet lag.

## 1.3 Important Preliminaries

There are two decisions that need to be made at the outset. Once the need for a physical and formal meeting has been determined, the first important task is to establish the purpose and the expected outcome or outcomes of the meeting. These must be clearly understood by all concerned, for without these the meeting is unlikely to prove valuable. If common objectives are shared prior to a meeting, the 'flow' will certainly be better.

Second, the people invited to attend must be given careful thought. (The number of participants will depend upon the organising body and the reason the meeting has been called). Is their presence essential? Can they afford the time? Will they be needed for all or only part of the meeting? Have all the stakeholders been considered? Will all the different interested groups be represented in the right balance? How many in total will be expected to attend? How will the attendees be informed of the purpose and expected outcome? How will they know what preparation (reading documents, obtaining information) is required of them?

## 7.2 THE MEETING PLACE

## 2.1 Choice of Location

Care must be taken when choosing and deciding on the location of the meeting place if meetings are to work with maximum efficiency and effect. You must be sure that all participants can access the meeting. Locations can vary depending on the country, available facilities and other circumstances. Neutral territory may be preferred if participants are divided for any reason. If some do not have their own vehicles, or a lift from others, then availability of public transport must be required. Humanitarian workers are often involved with physically disabled people who may need wheel-chair access, special toilet or other facilities.

Most meetings need private space. However, some are better held in public to allow discussion to be heard openly, so that members of the general community, not directly involved in the meeting, appreciate that agendas concerning themselves are not 'hidden'. Yet, open-air meetings can only be held with consideration for the weather or the need for a generator if certain visual aids or lighting are required. However, even indoor meetings may be halted by the noise of rain on a tin roof!

Outside or inside, weather conditions, temperature, mud, bad smells, lighting and generator (noise) can all be disruptive to meetings. If meetings are disturbed, the chairperson should obtain agreement from all participants, and then relocate or reschedule to ensure a productive continuation and outcome.

Consider the space:

- Big enough? Space for small group discussions?
- Columns in the way?
- Windows (use of wall space for maps, charts etc.)
- Proximity to noisy/smelly areas

- Traffic patterns and public transport
- Location of toilets
- Wall space and surface. Floor space for observers and wheelchair participants
- Electrical outlets
- Lighting
- Temperature control/fans

## 2.2 Room Layout

Meeting organisers should choose the layout that is best for the occasion so that all can hear the proceedings, see visual aids or engage in small group discussions as appropriate. Possible arrangements include:

- **Classroom style.** Seating arranged in straight lines with chairperson at the front.
- **Palais style.** Lines are curved to allow participants to see and hear each other more easily.
- **In-the-round.** A circular arrangement lets all have eye contact, and reduces the dominance of the chairperson.
- **Small group/cafe style.** Small individual tables place people in groups as in a café.
- **The doughnut.** Participants are seated in a rectangle or circle of tables with a central space.
- **The horseshoe.** All sit around a large central table. The chairperson may be at one end or in the centre of a long side.

**A Village Meeting**

Many serious, formal village-level meetings are **floor-based**. Floor seating may require mats for comfortable informality or formality.  A single mat provides a centre of focus.

Lastly, attention should be given to factors that can help or hinder the progress of the meeting. Some participants may be advised to reposition themselves in order to see visual aids more easily.

## 2.3  Domestic Arrangements

Provision of tea, coffee, lunch, sweets or water can all support a comfortable atmosphere that can help the business of the meeting proceed smoothly. Make sure that caterers are primed with break times and stress prompt service. For some meetings pens, paper or other materials such as folders may be needed or even expected. Where time must be saved, or numbers are large, the use of name tags for clothing or tables can speed introductions between unfamiliar individuals.

**7.3  THE AGENDA**

### 3.1 Notifying Participants

As well as indicating the organisation/structure of the meeting, one function of the agenda is to notify others of the forthcoming arrangements. The agenda can be posted on a notice board or distributed. This should be done at least one week before the meeting (at the latest, two days) to allow people to make arrangements for travel, obtaining/reading documents, personal work allocation, or cover. The agenda may need an accompanying explanation stating the purpose and expected outcome if it is the first of a series, or a single event. For the benefit of newcomers, the agenda can be accompanied by the minutes of the previous meeting. This will provide information about the kind of matters that are discussed, and the names of the other participants.

### 3.2 Document Identification

It is most important to date all documents and indicate the source or author. This is particularly significant during emergency situations, or when meetings concern security conditions that are changing rapidly. In these circumstances meetings can be frequent, so the current agenda and associated documents should be clearly identifiable. (Much time can be wasted, even dangerously, in trying to work out which document is current). Furthermore, participants may wish to contact the source in order to ensure adequate preparation or obtain clarification. So every document in a well-organised office will include a date, the sender's name, name(s) of recipient(s), and the action expected.

It is self evident that the agenda should indicate clearly the date, time, duration and place of the meeting. In addition, to help successors, or in anticipation of others having to retrieve documents in case of leave/sickness/end of contract/death, use of the 'Footer' can include the computer location where the document can be found. The footer can also be used to ensure that the name, date and page number occur on all pages of a multi-page document (that has a habit of losing first or last pages!)

### 3.3 Agenda Structure

There are several possible formats in which an agenda can be produced. Print should be large and items spaced to fill the page. (Try to leave enough space between points to allow participants to write their own comments). Information might include:

- **Date, time, and place** of meeting

- **The language medium** so expatriate time is not wasted

- Expected **duration** of the meeting

- In the case of a new meeting, **purpose and expected outcome**

- **Introductions** if necessary. Some meeting organisers list the names of those to whom the agenda has been sent

- **Approval of minutes** of previous meeting and corrections if necessary

- **Matters arising** from the minutes of the previous meeting. These should be of small importance. If major, they will be included in the main agenda

- **Items** should be carefully arranged in order to allow major discussions to be completed in an unhurried fashion. Contentious issues can be placed before a break to allow discussion time to be limited easily by the chairperson. Breaks can also be useful in helping cool the atmosphere if heated

- If **papers** are being provided and attached in support of items, this should be indicated alongside the item. This helps readers to prepare appropriately. (It is common but bad practice to table supporting papers at the time of the meeting. This makes no allowance for people reading at different speeds. If this is absolutely unavoidable, then the chairperson should allow time for reading. But the discussion is unlikely to be based on careful reflective thought as the time provided for reading may still be inadequate for some, and wasteful for others)

- Sometimes **a person** will be identified to deal with a particular matter, or to lead discussion on that topic. The item will also indicate this. Participants can be helpfully guided by showing approximate **discussion times** by the item; this draws attention to which matters are most or least important

- Sometimes **meetings may be divided** to allow participants (from different geographical areas, or with specific responsibilities) to attend clearly defined sections of the meeting e.g. "09.00 – 10.45 for those from the south and 11.15 – 13.00 hours for those from the north": the intervening break allows 'north' and 'south' to meet as well as providing some flexibility. In this way time wasting is minimised and the meeting can finish on time

- **Any Other Business.** This should not be used to encourage latecomers, and topics introduced at this late stage in a meeting should either be added to a future agenda, or only dealt with in emergency

- **Date, time and place of next meeting.** These details are most easily agreed when all participants are present, and temptations to offer phone calling to arrange details later should be resisted. (This is especially important in emergency situations when participants are likely to be spread in the field). It should be remembered that busy people are unlikely to be available at short notice and it can be difficult to make short-term future arrangements that are convenient for all. Difficulties can be avoided by planning meetings at the same time each week or month. This allows meetings to be fixed for long periods ahead. (Ideally, departments or organisations will agree an overall meetings programme and this can be most helpful where information generated from one type of meeting is required for another).

Look critically at the example of an agenda on the next page and suggest ways in which it could be improved. Can you spot what is missing? (See 3.2 for the answer).

*Staff Team Meeting*

**On**: Monday 9 February 2004

**In**: Seminar Room, Accra Office

**At**: 09.00 to 13.00 hours

**Distribution**: all programme staff in Head Quarters (HQ) and Field Offices.

**NB**. HQ staff are requested to attend entire meeting; Field Staff to attend 1st or 2nd part as appropriate although staff may attend whole meeting if they wish. Written suggestions re Items 4 and 7 should be sent to Samuel by 16 th

February.

## AGENDA

### Chair: Samuel Abouti

1. Welcome for new staff member, Affua Tamaklo, to HQ,

2. Minutes of the meeting of Monday 2 February 2004

3. Matters arising from the minutes

4. Possible joint training activities with Seva Ghana (20 minutes)

5. Catch-up education (see Paper 1. John Aduwasi to lead discussion) (45 minutes)     a) In south
   b) Single-parent women

6. Fire/First Aid Training (see Paper 2: attachment from last meeting)

**10.45 – 11.15 COFFEE BREAK**

7. Visit of Consortium President to Agriculture Training Programme

8. Proposal for Micro Finance Programme in the North (see Paper 3)
   a) Planning seminar
   b) Partners?
   c) Funding?

9. Any Other Business

10. Chairperson and Minutes Secretary for next meeting

Next Meeting in Field Office: date, time and place

## 4.1 The Role of the Chairperson

The chairperson or meeting facilitator has many responsibilities. She/he has to prepare the agenda after giving consideration to the purpose, intended outcome and the participants. But the participants or the group may not all share the same ideals and may be present for several reasons, such as:

- need to know
- job requirement - (they were <u>told</u> to go)
- legitimate concern and interest in the topic
- career advancement
- substitute for the "real" participant
- a good way to get out of other work
- love of learning
- some combination of the above and other reasons

As any chairperson knows, it is not easy to start the meeting on time, keep to time, and finish on time while achieving the task as well as satisfying individual and group needs. How many meetings start late because someone thinks that somebody may be coming – then they do not turn up! (Just multiply the time delay by the number of people present to find the total time wasted. Put a notional value on the average working hour of those concerned and you can see how much money and time have been wasted by late starts).

So start meetings exactly on time and after several meetings, latecomers will learn that you mean business. There are even gentle ways of making latecomers feel embarrassed, such as not leaving empty chairs, or apologizing for starting the meeting on time! Certainly, do not go over the business again for the benefit of those who could not travel with sufficient allowance for traffic etc, when others have met the deadline.

Start the meeting on a positive note by thanking participants for making the effort, and making sure that everybody knows the others, and why the meeting has been held. Take care to introduce new individuals. It is good practice to have a pack sent to newcomers so they know the framework of the business. What might be included in the pack? - mission statement of the group, dates of planned meetings, previous minutes, list of members. All this helps to get newcomers on board and active fast. This is particularly significant in the humanitarian world where contracts are short and turnover of staff is frequent.

It is strongly recommended to ask people to turn off telephones (especially if key personnel are likely to receive calls. One disturbing call can waste the time of many others).

The chairperson also needs to consider refreshment times in relation to agenda items. For longer, all-day sessions, the chairperson must start with a quick overview of the agenda including refreshment times. Try to avoid the distribution of coffee/tea, bananas, cakes etc while discussion is continuing, for obvious reasons. This does not save time, but rather leads to frustration and lack of concentration. Either stop the discussion, or take a complete break. For a short meeting, refreshments can be taken before for the benefit of those who have come long distances. There is an added advantage that latecomers miss the refreshments and not the meeting!

The matter of supporting papers has been mentioned in the previous section but it is worth repeating, that supporting papers will only be supportive if time before the meeting has been given to allow participants to read the material in a careful and reflective manner. Different people read at different speeds and the meeting is not the time for reading.

## 4.2    Observing Protocols and Voting
There are generally accepted and standard ways of conducting meetings that allow them to proceed smoothly and efficiently. Protocols for achieving this are there to help all concerned and should not be used to stifle discussion or progress. There are two main areas of concern. The first relates to the manner in which participants communicate, and the second deals with the ways of handling proposals and amendments.

Unless small group discussions are planned as part of the arrangements, participants should only speak one at a time, or else important contributions may be lost. The sensitive chairperson will be a student of body language and be aware, by keeping an eye on all the participants, when somebody wishes to add a talking point. A person wanting to join the discussion will usually lean forward, attempt to make eye contact with the chairperson, perhaps cough or move papers or water glass to attract attention, and raise a hand or an arm. The chairperson can indicate by nodding or pointing that the individual is free to speak. Sometimes many people wish to contribute to the discussion at about the same time. If the meeting is to be kept in control, the chairperson must ask participants to indicate intention to speak by raising a hand, then noting and keeping to a strict order of the contributors.

In larger assemblies, where participants are not all in direct sight of each other, it is better for the contributing individual to stand up before speaking. Then it is easier for all to be aware of the standing contributor whose voice will be heard more clearly throughout the meeting place. In even larger assemblies, it is usual for speakers to announce their name and affiliation. This will help the hearers appreciate the background of the comment, and will also be of benefit to the person recording the minutes. Normally a presenter should direct comments to the chairperson and not to some other individual in the audience. This serves to reduce the possibility of generally unheard local conversations (that in some cases could lead to personal attacks), and for the chairperson to redirect the topic to others if appropriate.

The second important protocol concerns proposals and amendments. It is easy for the meeting to become confused if these matters are not dealt with in an orderly manner. For example, someone proposes that an agricultural project should be started in the north of the country next year. This proposal contains three ingredients: the nature of the programme, the location, and the time. Immediate voting becomes difficult when people may not agree/disagree with each of these components. Then somebody wishes to amend the proposal to suggest that the project would be more appropriate in the south, while a third person feels strongly that the project should commence this year and not next. Yet another person thinks that, if there is to be a project in the south, the proposal should be amended to education and not agriculture. Discussion becomes heated; people reiterate their views not wanting their point to be lost. At some point, the chairperson must call a halt and allow voting to reach a democratic decision.

So how does the chairperson 'unpack' all the points? Experience has shown that it is better to vote first on the amendments before obtaining a decision on the main issue.
One way of dealing with the complications above is to vote on the issues in the following order:

a) Is a project to begin this year, or next? (I.e. When could resources/funding/capacity be available?)
b) Should the project be in the north or the south of the country? (Where is the greater need? Is an initial needs assessment required?)
c) Then the main proposal can be presented. Should the project be in agriculture or education?

**Before voting**, and if time allows after the chairperson has clarified the decision point, further discussion, for clarification only, can be allowed. At this stage it is usually wise to allow a person to speak only once, otherwise some may attempt to force opinion by force of voice! Often, at this stage, there are some who would like to change the order of voting. But if two people sit on a horse, only one can be in front, and it is essential for the chairperson to keep the lead. This does not mean that the most senior person must always be in the chair.

**The voting** follows by a show of hands (or use of ballot papers in large general and formal situations), recording those who are for, against, or abstaining. It is important to note abstentions, as a simple majority of 'fors' may not truly reflect the will of the meeting if the number of abstentions is high. In fact, the chairperson needs to make clear, before the voting takes place, what is required for an acceptable majority decision.
Give thought to the **voting process.** In delicate situations voting should be anonymous as voters can be influenced in their decision if they know others can see which way they are voting. Furthermore, even in democratic situations, it may not be desirable for junior staff to be seen to vote against the opinion of their seniors.

Once the voting has taken place, no further discussion is appropriate. The decisions have been taken and there is neither need nor use in allowing a minority, who may feel aggrieved, to have the opportunity to reiterate their position.

### 4.3 Managing the Meeting
The work of the chairperson is far from easy and practice is required to find the balance between encouraging the quiet ones, limiting the outspoken, and not taking the opportunity of the dominant position in the meeting also to dominate the discussion. The latter is particularly difficult when the chairperson may be better informed on a topic than others. Many meetings should be run on democratic lines and all opinions carefully heard and discussed. At other times the chairperson may need to be authoritative, taking decisions in a required time, controlling content, or disciplining unacceptable behaviour. Issues need to be highlighted and summarised so that all are kept in the conceptual arena. Special care and patience must be given to those who may be communicating in their second or third language.

**When numbers are large** and time is short, there may be a need to ask participants to speak only once on a topic. This can be particularly important when interpretation is required.

**When the atmosphere is** most energetic, or even **heated**, sometimes it is better to postpone the decision-making process. Decisions are best taken when tempers are cool and calm. In extreme cases it may be necessary to take the matter to a higher forum for a decision to be reached.

**When some participants are not participating**, give pointed opportunity by requesting views from individuals or organisations. And give encouragement to the responses. Some participants hold back because they:

- Fear rejection
- Feel pressure from other more senior people
- Lack preparation
- Have an incomplete understanding of what has gone before

**When actions have been decided**, identify the person responsible and clarify the action required, and by when. Sometimes it is good to provide a 'supporter' who also checks that action has been taken!

This is an oversimplification of meeting facilitation as any chairperson knows, and there are many impediments to the process. Several techniques are used to disrupt meetings. They can occur at any time, often unexpectedly, and the chairperson must be prepared for:
- Personal attacks
- Sleeping
- Abusive speech/behaviours
- Filibusters (a person who uses, or even abuses, procedures to delay the process)
- Those who just say "NO" to any issue (Nay sayers)
- Latecomers

**The smart chairperson will:**

- Identify potential problems before they occur - talk through the agenda with participants beforehand if possible.
- Take pre-emptive action
- Keep calm and not panic.
- Maintain a sense of humour
- Be willing to change to a better plan

**If matters become really serious then:**

- Deal with it outside the room.
- Call a break if necessary
- Set up a group task force
- Enrol the help of other participants

- Set up a committee or small group to represent participants' particular needs or interests
- Remain neutral. Do not take sides generally, but be prepared to take assertive authority if the occasion demands

If confronted with **complete disorder and disruption,**

- Never get upset or emotional yourself
- Isolate one element and try to deal with it to reduce the overall temperature
- Agree before resuming
- Call for a few minutes of complete silence
- Call a short break
- Put the item aside until later
- Abandon the meeting

**Out of Control**

The **good chairperson** is creative and will:

- Always remain in control of time
- Actively stimulate creative thinking
- Personally contribute new ideas or steer the                     discussion in new or unusual directions
- Find new ways of looking at things
- Consider novel approaches and give them a chance
- Aim to solve problems, not tread familiar pathways

## 4.4    Concluding the Meeting

**A well-directed meeting will have:**

- Focused betobjectives ter on its

- Fostered          more          constructive discussions

- Led to a thorough review so that *ad hoc* decisions are          avoided

- Encouraged     all     sides     of     the argument or case to be

At the **end of the meeting** the chairperson should:

- Review the key decisions
- Indicate issues for future discussion

- Fix time and place of next meeting. Remember that this is particularly important in emergency situations
- Thank the participants for coming
- Declare that the meeting has ended. (If this sounds a little heavy or obvious, wish participants something pleasant so that the meeting starts and finishes on a positive note, even if the middle part has been difficult to handle!

## 7.5  MEETING RECORDS

### 5.1 Types of Minutes

Without a written record of the proceedings the intentions of the meeting will almost certainly be lost. If minutes are not kept, hours of time may be wasted by rediscussion at a later date, or argument occurs about what was actually agreed. Several different kinds of minutes can be recorded. At one extreme there can be a full record of all the discussion on almost a word for word basis. This is usually unnecessary: ideas develop and opinions change during the discussion. Progress and improvement develop from a conflict of views, and usually there is little need for or value in recording the modifications of views as they occur.

So the group or the chairperson needs to agree the nature of the records. These can be:

- A **word for word account**. This may only have value in reporting a highly contentious and significant discussion of extreme importance e.g. when two political or warring parties are being brought together, or when a prisoner is interviewed by the police. In such situations it is best to use a tape recorder for later transcription. But be consistent when deciding to use first or second names, and the name of the organisation

- If a **relatively full account** is needed in a situation less important than the above, just the main arguments can be recorded that led to a particular conclusion or decision being taken

- Most usual are **minutes** that only record attendance, apologies for absence, decisions and required actions, and details of the next meeting; this is sufficient for most routine situations

- Of great value when time is short and people are under pressure is the **tabular form of minutes**. This method is under-utilised. The table can be completed during the course of the meeting, photocopied and distributed immediately. The table includes the key agenda points, a required action, who is responsible, and the agreed date by which the action will be completed.

| Minutes of Programme Staff Meeting: Accra HQ on 04.11.2011 at 09-11.00 hours | | | |
|---|---|---|---|
| Agenda item | Action required | Person responsible | To be completed by: |

| 3. NGO Vehicles | Replace tyres on car | John Brown | 04.12.2011 |
|---|---|---|---|
| 5. Budget | Draft WatSan proposal | Sally Baidoo | 11.12.2011 |
| Etc.......................... | | | |
| Michael Wahid (Chair) | | | |

- For ease of reference the numbering of Minute Items should correspond exactly with the numbers used in the Agenda.

- Number all pages. The format '1 of 5, 2 of 5 etc' is useful as it makes clear if pages are missing or duplicated.

## 5.2 Distribution of Minutes

Minutes are best circulated within 24 hours of the meeting. Rapid distribution gives maximum time for actions to be effected while the matter is still fresh in mind. Sending out the minutes with the next agenda just before the next meeting is common practice but is usually too late to be effective.

A useful way to be sure that minutes are distributed to all attendees is to ask all participants to sign an attendance sheet giving postal or email addresses. If the meeting has been interpreted, then the minutes will also need to be translated before distribution.

For meetings that may have a highly significant impact, it is sometimes useful to indicate that minutes are in draft form until they have been agreed. Another approach is to send out minutes to a limited group for feed-back or correction before they are finally distributed to the wider audience. If this is done, the process must be clearly transparent and the meeting should be informed before this occurs.

## 7.6.  CHECK - LIST OF ACTIONS REQUIRED

### 6.1 Decisions and Actions to be Taken

- Determine the purpose(s) and expected outcome(s)
- Decide who should be invited and the total attendance anticipated
- Book the location; check audio-visual aids and materials required (flip chart, pencils/ball pens, pads, name labels etc)
- Arrange refreshments (water, sweets, tea, coffee, biscuits, lunch arrangements), and decide their timing in relation to the agenda
- Draft agenda
- Select a secretary to distribute the agenda and take minutes. (The most useful person will be competent and have a knowledge of the subject)
- Prepare papers to be attached to agenda items for precirculation
- Finalise the agenda and circulate. Post a copy on a notice board

- Arrive at the meeting place early to check room or space is available and that domestic arrangements (audio-visual aids/name tags/seating) are in order
- Start the meeting exactly on time
- Ask all to turn off mobile telephones

## 6.2 Actions to Avoid

Many problems in meeting organisation arise from leaving decisions and actions too late for general comfort. So avoid:

- Delays in making decisions about the need for, purpose and expected outcomes of meetings
- Leaving bookings for rooms, domestic arrangements, visual aids until the last minute
- Presenting supporting papers at the meeting. People cannot read them while concentrating on the matters under discussion. If extreme circumstances force papers to be tabled, chairpersons must allow time for them to be read making special allowance for those whose native language is not that used in the paper. Tabled papers can cause confusion, disruption, and raise suspicions that an item is being 'bulldozed'. To ensure that papers are always  precirculated, either with or even before the agenda, allow time for electrical/photocopier/postal and other failures.

A good meeting needs concentration and interruptions must be minimized.

- Don't be sidetracked
- Beware of meetings within meetings. Insist that participants speak only once to a topic if individuals are getting repetitive or too dominant • Beware of digressions

### 7.7  A FINAL WORD TO PARTICIPANTS

Each time a meeting is convened, ask yourself:

- Is it really necessary to attend? (Make a conscious decision about attending)
- What can I contribute?
- What can I get from it?

Come to definite answers before you set out. And be determined to go to the meeting on time, not late! If you arrive early, then use the time to network and the time will not be wasted.

- Read supporting papers in advance
- Prepare your contribution controlling your nerves
- Annotate any relevant documents and make notes as necessary
- Plan questions that you will need to ask
- Note who will attend
- Put information over in a way that is explicit, accurate and precise
- If your name is put against an action point, then take seriously the responsibility to follow up with action, and complete the task in time

**Do not**
- Monopolize the conversation
- Talk to the person next to you during the meeting
- Constantly interrupt others
- Become emotional or argumentative to no good purpose
- Make it difficult to stick to the allotted time
- Appear unprepared, undisciplined or a troublemaker
- Digress pointlessly from the topic


## 8. How to Plan a PowerPoint Presentation

(This section assumes a basic knowledge of computing and Microsoft Office packages in addition to Microsoft PowerPoint)

### 9.1 Introduction
Anybody in a professional position may be asked to make a formal presentation to colleagues or to 'outside' audiences. How we present our talk can influence the way in which our ideas are received, and the impact that they can have on the recipients. This is particularly important when making a presentation of a proposal to a donor requesting funding for a project. A poor presentation of a good suggestion may be wrongly interpreted as a poor idea. There are simple guidelines for helping presenters to make the best impact.

Presentations have advantages and disadvantages compared with other forms of communication. They allow emphasis to be made of key points in a subject, attract interest, place emphasis on the 'U-value' ('you'), and the transfer of new ideas/data, summaries and enthusiasm. (Enthusiasm needs to be pitched just above the level of the audience as both disinterest and over enthusiasm can have depressant effects on hearers). Supporting documents have a helpful role. However, presentations obviously demand that all concerned will be present at the same in the same place and wanting to hear what you have to tell. Part of your task is to make and keep people interested. A significant advantage is that, having come to the presentation, people are now in a position to listen to and discuss your ideas.

### 9.2 What can be presented
PowerPoint presentations are useful in many situations. These include:
- an automated, continuously running show to accompany an **exhibition**, which can be displayed on a computer or larger screen depending on audience size. It can include music and video clips
- giving an account of your **holiday**/travels to family and friends
- selling a **product**, too large or small to actually demonstrate, to a customer
- presenting **results** of research to a scientific/social/medical group
- introducing a new **concept** to a group of colleagues for discussion
- making a **proposal** to donors for funding
- reporting project **progress** to management

- entertainment

## 9.3 Aspects for consideration in planning

**a) The duration of the talk.** Always aim to talk for less time than scheduled because most people tend to run out of time not matter! Make sure you also allow time for comments or questions. If your slot is 20 minutes, plan for 15. If you are a beginner and need to practise your talk, do so out loud because generally we speak more slowly than we read.

**b) The type of audience and knowledge level of others.** If the audience is of mixed ability, be sure to cater for both ends of the spectrum. Start with the familiar before moving to unfamiliar ground. If you begin with unfamiliar material you are in danger of losing your audience from the outset. "I am going to explain why our hands get cold and sweaty, and our stomach turns to jelly when we stand up in front of an audience" is a better way of starting than saying, "Today I will cover the structure and function of the sympathetic nervous system in order to help us understand our response to stress".

**c) U-value** (This relates to 'you'). Show early in the talk that the topic is relevant to the hearers. During the introduction let the audience know that the topic will be valuable for them. E.g. "All of us need to approach donors for funds and PowerPoint presentations can be a powerful tool in achieving success".

**d) Use of verbal language.** Will you need an interpreter? If so, you must reduce your material and the number of slides by more than half because translation more than doubles the time taken to present a talk. Interpretation sometimes needs to be repeated or expanded for clarification. It is possible to make a presentation using only pictures, diagrams and cartoons as these can convey a message sometimes better than words where language comprehension is limited.

A common but inappropriate device for checking that people can both hear you and understand is to ask the audience at the back if they can hear. If they cannot – they will not respond. If they cannot understand, they are unlikely to admit so in public. That is clearly a waste of time and breath. More usefully start with some quick humour. If the audience laughs: continue. If they do not laugh, speak more slowly and try again.

**e) Use of body language.** It is important for your body to face and be in connection with the hearers. You need to face the front to make eye contact with the audience, not the screen for most of the time. (You do need to check quickly that the slide you are discussing is the one on the screen!). If you are controlling your presentation with a laptop on the desk in front of you, make sure you point to the screen which the audience can see and not your computer screen which they cannot observe.

**f) An interactive talk, or just one-way delivery.** There are many tools available to the experienced presenter to make the presentation interactive and this is a useful way to hold audience attention. One technique is to start by asking the audience to offer questions that they expect to be answered during the period. These can be listed on the board or chart. Then you give your talk just as intended. The audience has been converted from passive listeners to active learners, waiting to see if you cover their aspect. At the end, check through the questions to ensure all have been covered. Be warned. Interaction needs to be controlled or it can take up too much time.

**g) Keeping audience attention.** Especially during a long presentation you may need to insert ways of refocusing the attention of the meeting. Techniques include the use of cartoons, introducing a short question which you ask the audience to answer by discussion with a neighbour, a picture, a photograph (especially if one of the chairperson!) or music. An unfailing device is to insert a short video clip, or break a long talk into parts with a short film in between. Every member of the audience will prefer to watch a moving picture rather than a still one. Animation of slides can also be used but excessive use of text swirling and sliding about on the screen becomes boring or even annoying. Limit its use to make a significant point, otherwise every point becomes over emphasised.

**h)** Does your talk need to **link with other presentations** in the programme? If your presentation is one in a bigger programme, a reference to an earlier slot or a later one will help to bind the programme together. A professional speaker will have taken the trouble to contact other presenters before the day to see how talks can be linked to underpin or extend other sessions in the programme.

**i) Supporting documentation.** The best way to ensure that your message is taken away from the meeting is to provide supporting documentation. This can be in the form of a manuscript of your discourse but there is a danger that recipients will spend time reading when you would prefer them to watch. Others may relax thinking that the document can be read later. A useful way is to provide a print of your slides in a way which allows people to add their own notes and comments. Under File/Print you will find a window in the bottom left-hand corner which allows you to print up to six slides on a page with enough white space for notes to be added. Explore this window and the several choices it offers.

**j) Summary and conclusions.** Many presenters finish their talk with a slide that acknowledges the work and contribution of others. That is the final message that the audience will take away. So if you need to thank others, do so at the beginning, or after the introduction. Your last slide should not be a 'thank you' slide. Just say "thank you" if you think your audience has been patient but let your last slide be your key message. It is the conclusion of your talk and it can stay on the screen throughout the question time to increase its impact.

### 9.4 Structure and sequence

There are several different ways of structuring information; you need to choose the one which is the best aid to memory for your audience. As most people can remember three or four points, but not five or more, this will dictate the number of sections you use. Each section may be subdivided, but the same rule applies.

Please do a small exercise. There are 120 ways to arrange five sentences but here are just eight examples:

<table>
<tr><td></td><td>The enemy approached</td></tr>
<tr><td></td><td>The enemy ran away</td></tr>
</table>

1. I was on sentry duty
    I opened fire
    It was a lucky escape

2. I opened fire
    I was on sentry duty

It was a lucky escape
The enemy approached
The enemy ran away

3.  It was a lucky escape
I was on sentry duty
I opened fire
The enemy ran away
The enemy approached


.      4. The enemy ran away  I
was on sentry duty
I opened fire
It was a lucky escape
The enemy approached

5.  I was on sentry duty
The enemy approached
I opened fire
The enemy ran away
It was a lucky escape

6.  The enemy approached
It was a lucky escape
The enemy ran away
I was on sentry duty
I opened fire

7.  The enemy ran away  I was on
sentry duty
It was a lucky escape
The enemy approached
I opened fire

8.  It was a lucky escape
The enemy ran away
The enemy
approached
I opened fire
I was on sentry duty

Look at these groups and decide which is the best for telling the story. Of course some novels are written in a way which sets out a problem then recapitulates to explain the events which led to this situation. (e.g. "I opened my eyes and looked down the barrel of a gun!") While a highly skilled narrator can do this, most of us need a safer approach. So perhaps you chose number 5. Why? It gives a chronological account – I was on sentry duty AND THEN the enemy approached AND THEN and so on. However, there is another structure hidden here which is invaluable for any form of presentation, report or even an impromptu short speech.

Group 5 illustrates:
- a situation
- a problem
- a solution (or solutions
- the effect
- a comment

Try it out for yourself. Think of any topic. Malaria, perhaps.

Malaria kills about three million people every year, mostly children **(the situation)**. The parasite is developing resistance to anti-malarial drugs and the mosquitoes are becoming resistant to insecticides **(the problem).**
We must find a way to reverse resistance or develop better ways of treatment **(possible solutions)**
In these ways, we can combat one of the world's worst diseases **(the effect).**
In achieving this we will have to feed three million more people every year **(a comment).**

This example uses only single sentences but it could be expanded into paragraphs, sections, or chapters. It can be adapted for a short or a long PowerPoint presentation with the first four headings giving the themes of the four sections of your talk. For some purposes it may only be necessary to use the situation, the problem and possible solutions with comments after each possibility.

To summarise this section, the structure of the presentation is important and it should follow a logical sequence in not more than three or four sections. The arrangement can be based on:

- a chronological sequence
- describing the end situation, comparing it with the beginning, reviewing possible causes to explain the difference
- using situations, problems, solutions, effects and comments
- answers to a list of questions: how, when, what and why etc

**9.5 The Slides**
This is the central focus of the presentation. There are good slides and bad ones. Slides must be limited to an average of no more than **one a minute**. They should be: - visual aids and not visual distractions
- simple and clear
- bullet points not full text
- cartoons, pictures, graphs and charts as all have a place

You will appear unprofessional and a time waster if you arrive at the rostrum and start by asking the chairperson, "How do I turn the projector on? How do I turn the lights off? Is there a pointer? Is the microphone working? Can you help me focus this?" Then you start showing the wrong slides, or keep the audience waiting while you click through endless computer windows in search of your slides. We have all seen this happen too many times.

Here are some guidelines which aid the production of good slides and polished professional presentations:

a) **Get to the meeting place early** and make sure you know where all the switches are and how to work the lights, microphone, pointer and computer

b) **Put your slide set on the Desk Top** so one click starts your presentation immediately. A white screen is disturbing, so start and end your slide set with a totally black slide. This allows you to turn on equipment without 'giving away' your beginning prematurely. After your final black slide, you may add some others which could be useful in the question period. Do not be tempted to show these if they are not relevant to the discussion. All audiences and chairpersons love speakers who finish early

c) **Avoid standard slide formats that confuse** with slashes and flares, pictures of flowers or animals. They distract.

d) **Adopt a standard format** for all your slide presentations as this will allow you to mix slide sets while still giving the impression that the sequence has been put together just for that occasion. Do not number slides for this reason. You may like to put a logo on the first slide, but it is not necessary to add a logo to every slide

e) **Change slide format only if the change is significant.** E.g. you may like to change the background colour as you move from one section to the next. Light-coloured text on a dark background is comfortable, so you could change from dark blue, to green to brown, and then finish with your key message on a splash of yellow and red.

f) **Be consistent with text sizes and fonts** for headings and bullet points. As a guide keep within 7 lines and 7 words to a line. Avoid wasted repetition of the same words or phrases on a slide. Use lower case apart from headings. All words in capital letters seems like shouting. Spell-check your slides and remove every single unnecessary word. What should the following slide say? Then add a picture.


Good fresh high quality fish just caught sold          here in this
                                  shop.


g) **Never put up extensive text which you read aloud.** This is insulting to an audience who may read better than you or at a different speed. If you must display a document, make sure it is legible and leave the slide in silence while others read. But bullet points are always better if possible

h) **Never put up a table** parts of which you ask to be ignored. Usually data is collected in tables but differences need to be shown by diagrams. Few people are sufficiently skilled to glance at a table and immediately see trends and differences. Differences in time MUST be shown by line diagrams or other graphs; differences in amounts MUST be shown by histograms or pie diagrams. MS Excel is brilliant at converting tables to charts with all axes labelled and these can be immediately transferred to PowerPoint slides

## 9.6 Summary of Tips for Good Presentations

1. Get to the room or hall early to set up equipment, and to make sure you know how to work everything: projector, computer, lights, pointer and microphone
2. Make eye contact with the audience and smile
3. Outline the structure of the talk in the introduction. Change passive listening to active learning
4. Develop a clear structure in 3 or 4 sections only
5. Use graphs and charts not numbers
6. Make gaps between sections; change visual aid style/format only for significance
7. Maintain a logical sequence
8 Use visual aids not visual distractions
9 Start with the familiar before progressing to the unfamiliar
10. Keep the attention of audience by U-value, varying voice, cartoons, relevant examples and surprises
11. Keep to time. Later, watch a video recording of yourself for punishment!
12. Summarise and finish with your key message (not thanks)

**NO!**

| Year | Govt. Military Expenditure (GM) (%GDP) | Effect of GM on Public Investment (% GDP) | Using Marginal Product of Investment on GDP | | | Using Average Product of Investment on GDP | | | |
| | | | Drop in GDP Growth Rate (%) | Estimated Lost GDP | | ICOR | Drop in GDP Growth Rate (%) | Estimated Lost GDP | |
| | | | | Rs. Mn (1996) | (Per cent GDP) | | | Rs. Mn (1996) | (Per cent GDP) |
|---|---|---|---|---|---|---|---|---|---|
| 1984 | 1.61 | -0.79 | 0.07 | 283 | 0.07 | 5.11 | 0.15 | 615 | 0.15 |
| 1985 | 3.46 | -5.21 | 0.47 | 1,966 | 0.45 | 4.81 | 1.08 | 4,527 | 1.03 |
| 1986 | 5.41 | -9.90 | 0.89 | 3,913 | 0.86 | 5.53 | 1.79 | 7,913 | 1.73 |
| 1987 | 5.79 | -10.81 | 0.97 | 4,476 | 0.97 | 16.05 | 0.67 | 3,126 | 0.68 |
| 1988 | 4.83 | -8.51 | 0.77 | 3,579 | 0.75 | 6.44 | 1.01 | 4,697 | 0.99 |
| 1989 | 3.49 | -6.30 | 0.48 | 2,282 | 0.47 | 9.85 | 0.55 | 2,633 | 0.54 |
| 1990 | 4.54 | -7.81 | 0.70 | 3,431 | 0.67 | 3.60 | 2.17 | 10,607 | 2.06 |
| 1991 | 4.21 | -7.01 | 0.63 | 3,279 | 0.61 | 4.96 | 1.41 | 7,446 | 1.39 |
| 1992 | 4.23 | -7.07 | 0.64 | 3,457 | 0.61 | 5.67 | 1.25 | 6,824 | 1.21 |
| 1993 | 4.16 | -6.90 | 0.62 | 3,518 | 0.59 | 3.89 | 1.89 | 10,697 | 1.79 |
| 1994 | 4.41 | -7.50 | 0.67 | 4,086 | 0.64 | 4.80 | 1.56 | 9,565 | 1.50 |
| 1995 | 5.24 | -9.49 | 0.85 | 5,484 | 0.81 | 4.72 | 2.01 | 12,974 | 1.94 |
| 1996 | 6.02 | -11.37 | 1.02 | 6,915 | 0.99 | 6.45 | 1.76 | 12,045 | 1.73 |

**Yes!**

| | UNHCR | WFP | CARF | RC | MIN/INT | N/TRANS WATER | .efugees |
|---|---|---|---|---|---|---|---|
| *FOOD* | X | X | X | X | X | | X |
| *WATER* | X | | | | | X | X |
| *SANITATION* | X | | | | | | X |
| *SECURITY* | X | | | X | | | X |
| *SHELTER* | X | | | | X | | X |
| *LOGISTICS* | | X | X | | X | | X |
| *EDUCATION* | | | | | | | |

# 9. How to Prepare a Report

**Compiled by Lia van Ginneken**
**(www.networklearning.org) REPORT WRITING IN GENERAL**
• Preparation for report writing
• The actual writing of the report • The different parts of your report

**THE PROJECT PROGRESS REPORT**
• About Project Progress Report (PPRs)
• Checklist for writing a Project Progress Report (PPR) • Flash reports

## Introduction

Reports are important management tools for influencing future actions. Through reports, information can be shared and consequently lessons learned.

However, good report writing is not easy and it is very time consuming. In addition, if a report is not easy to read, it probably will not be read at all.

In these guidelines attention is paid to report writing in general and, in particular, to the Project Progress Report. If the ideas or words being used in these guidelines are not familiar to you, please look at the manual 'How to build a good small NGO', chapters 3 through 6, on the www.networklearning.org site, or ask for more explanation by e-mailing to: ginneken.noordman@wxs.nl.

_________________________________________________ REPORT

**WRITING IN GENERAL**

_________________________________________________

## Preparation for report writing

**Subject:** Decide which kind of information needs to be in the report. Be as precise as possible. For donors, four types of information are usually needed:

1. What the results are so far of the implementation of the project (impact development information)
2. Which activities have been implemented so far. Is this according to the project proposal? (Activity implementation information)
3. How was the money spent? (finance/budget information) 4. Information about the project staff.

**Purpose:** Determine what the purpose of the report is. Is it to inform others so that they become interested in the project? Or is it a presentation of the results of the project to e.g. your donor?

**Layout:** Check whether the report needs to be written in a compulsory layout (e.g. type of paper, headings footings, standardised form, etc.)

**Target group:** Determine who the readers of the report will be. The contents of the report need to be adjusted to the people who will read it. E.g. how much information do they already have about the project?

In a progress report with the purpose to keep readers informed, only the latest information is needed. If you want to present the project to a potential donor, or you want to inform other outsiders, you need to be more elaborate in explaining where the project is all about. The target group will also determine the level of language you need to use.

**Structure:** Check how the contents of the report need to be arranged.

**Length:** Determine the maximum number of pages in consultation with whoever commissioned the report.

**Time span:** Check out when the report needs to be ready. Then make a time plan for yourself for writing the report (date for completing the first draft, date for having it checked by a senior colleague etc).

**The actual writing of the report**

*Collect the information needed.*
Important sources are: reports, notes which have been written earlier, books, information from your monitoring system, interviews with staff/target groups etc.

*Arrange your information in a logical way and take care the structure is well balanced (see section 9).*
The way the report is divided determines the structure. Make use of chapters, paragraphs, sub-paragraphs. Chapters need to be roughly the same length. Paragraphs should be a logical subdivision of the chapters. Keep each short and make sure that one paragraph covers one subject.

*Write in the language of your reader* – not childish or over-sophisticated. Avoid long and complicated sentences (not longer than 15 –20 words). Take care that the report is easy readable without reference to other literature. If needed, use footnotes to explain certain concepts/ideas.

*Try not to make any spelling mistakes.*
If you are writing on a computer, use the spell-check.

*Make sure the layout is well organised.*
The reader will give up quickly if it takes too much effort to follow the line of
your argument. Make sure that there is enough space between the lines,
paragraphs etc.

*Check the result by asking the following:*
1. Does the report answer the questions raised by whoever
   commissioned it?
2. Is the structure logical and well balanced? Is the order of
   the topics correct?
3. Have the pages been numbered and is this according to the
   Index?
4. Has somebody else read the report and been asked for
   feedback, before you send it to the person who
   commissioned it?

**The different parts of your report**

Depending on the purpose of the report, you can choose different ways of arranging
the content. The following division is one of the most common:

**The cover:** (preferably of a heavier quality of paper than the rest of the report). On
the cover it should mention:

- The title of the report;
- The sub-title (if appropriate);
- The name of the author(s);
- The date of the presentation of the report.

Depending on whether your report is for internal or external use, you can
mention your own organisation and/or the organisation for whom the report
is written, e.g. the donor organisation.

**The title page:** this is not always necessary. Usually the information of the
cover page is repeated. If applicable, information on copyrights, distribution
etc. could be mentioned here.

**The Index:** this should be a separate page on which the chapters and
paragraphs are listed next to the appropriate page number. Only the first
page number of each chapter is listed.

**The foreword:** this is not always needed; it depends on the type of report.
In the foreword issues are mentioned which are not essential to the contents
of the report, like: words of thanks, for whom the report was written, by
whom and why etc.

**The summary:** the summary is important because not everybody has time to read the whole report. In the summary, the most important points are presented:

- the reason why the report was written;
- the questions which are to be raised (problem statement);
- the solutions;
- the arguments used for the solutions;
- important conclusions and advice.

**The main text of the report:** The main text is most commonly divided into the following chapters:

**Introduction:** this indicates the structure of the report. In the introduction often issues are described which are obvious to the writer of the report, but not to the reader. By reading the introduction, the reader should understand what exactly the report is all about; which topics are included, which are not and why; how the information was obtained; why the report was written; what the aims of the report are (e.g. is the report written to present information, to advise, to evaluate?) etc.

**Clarification of the problem statement:** this chapter explains why the information is needed, which information is needed and how the information obtained will be used. (Or what the problem is, why the problem needs to be solved and which information is needed to be able to solve the problem).

**Methodology:** a short description of how the information was obtained (methodology).

**Results:** graphs and charts are always more helpful than tables of numbers. Provide an interpretation and description of the information obtained.

**Conclusions of the results**

**Recommendations:** it is better to make recommendations for each conclusion or group of conclusions.

**Annexes:** if information or explanations which take up a lot of space and attention are in the text then they can make the report difficult to read. This type of information is better put in the Annexes. For example: a literature list (references to literature used in the report), detailed explanations, examples, drawings, maps, list of abbreviations etc.

Annexes should be numbered and should have a title. In the main report, references should be made to the annexes when needed. Annexes are also listed in the Index.


THE PROJECT PROGRESS REPORT

**About Project Progress Reports (PPRs)**

Extra attention should be paid to the Project Progress Report. A project manager should prepare them on a regular basis. They are often for internal use and are based on your monitoring system (see 'How to build a good small NGO' chapter 6).

The information will help you to know how the project is going. You can share this information with colleagues or beneficiaries; you can discuss its contents with more senior management or with other units and you can feed the lessons learned back into the next round of planning. These project progress reports will also form the basis for your reports to governments and donors. (see above under 'Report writing in general').

Project Progress Reports may be produced monthly, quarterly, annually or according to any timetable that is agreed on. They may be structured or presented in a number of different ways. By standardising the structure of the report they will be easier to complete. More importantly, comparison can be made between reports over time.

The basic layout of a progress report should include the following items:

- the activity or work area being considered;
- a time schedule for the period you are reporting on and completed activities;
- targets which have been reached during the period;
- budget and actual expenditures (inputs and costs);
- problems/constraints experienced and management action required.

In addition there may be details about revenue and manpower, and reference to activities related to the project but not directly under the project management control.

The reports usually contain a mixture of narrative comment and quantitative data. They should make clear what was planned and what was achieved or when targets were not set, what was achieved in the same period the year before.

PPRs provide an important source of information over time about activities and their outputs. Their usefulness will depend on the regularity with which they are completed and their quality. The common problems of PPRs are that they are too lengthy, with poor or incomplete coverage of the key issues. They are often largely descriptive, rather than focussed on performance and management action.

**Checklist for writing a Project Progress Report (PPR)**

a. **Objectives.** A PPR should refer to all the objectives of the project components reported on and on the outputs.

b. **Indicators.** Progress should be reported on the basis of indicators which are described in the project proposal. PPRs should use the same indicators throughout the project period. This way, performance over a long time period can be analysed.

c. **Targets.** For each indicator there should be a target and preferably the targets should be all of the same consistency: e.g. all targets are (bi) annual. This makes them easier to compare and interpret.

d. **Narrative content.** The purpose of writing PPRs is to identify progress towards producing outputs and meeting objectives. It should be output-oriented. In practice, many PPRs tell what has been done in the style of a diary. Though often interesting, this is less helpful.

e. **Management analysis.** This should focus on actions that require the attention of more senior management, or other units, divisions or departments outside of the control of the project manager.

The purpose of the analysis is to improve and support the implementation of the project. Specific attention should be paid to distinguishing between the following types of possible problems which may have an impact on the achievement of the project:

- objectives
- project design weakness
- accuracy of planning and budgeting
- resource constraints
- coordinating problems
- management problems internal to the organisation
- adverse external environmental factors

Understanding the nature of the problems being faced will help ensure that appropriate action is being taken.

**Flash reports**

Such reports should be limited to one page only and are designed to highlight key issues while requiring the minimum amount of paper work. The flash report is ideally suited to be a monthly update for transmission through a fax machine.

<u>**NB It is essential that all documents include the name of the author and the date. If this is not done much time can be wasted in trying to locate the author for further discussion, or in trying to ascertain which document of several drafts is the current one.**</u>

<u>**When reporting on emergency situations it may also be necessary to add the time as several reports may be made during the course of the same day.**</u>

# 10. How to Control Your Time

(This section is partly based on a workshop on "Time Management" organised for the British Council in Sri Lanka by Keith Ellis)

## 12.1 Introduction
If you could add three hours to your week how would you spend them? Would you:
- do more work?
- spend more time with your family?
- read a book?
- go for a walk or follow some fitness activity?
- chat to friends over a drink?
- do something you have always wanted to do but have never had the time for it? - just dream? - other?

If you follow these guidelines thoughtfully, prepared to change yourself from a *Human Being* to a *Human Doing*, most people in work can gain several more hours in their week by managing their time better.

Time is money. Suppose you wait with 19 other committee members for 1 hour in anticipation of another colleague arriving for a meeting. What has that cost? If the average salary of your work mates is 400,000 UGS a month, that is 20,000 a working day or about 2,500 an hour. Between the twenty of you 50,000 UGS have been lost. Now multiply this by all the meetings in a year which start late plus the appointments made but not kept, and the times you came to work late or left early (especially on Friday afternoons), and you arrive at a huge sum which has been stolen from your employer. In addition, your own time has been wasted never to be regained. However, back in the office, much more time is lost for other reasons. Taming your time will help you to be more successful. It will help you to operate more effectively, and it will save you from stress and even burnout. It will also give you extra time.

> *"1) A Public officershall have strict regard to the working hours. He or She shall not come late to office meetings and Official functions without reasonable cause (The Code of Conduct for the Uganda Public Service, 2006)."*

You will need to be aware of:
- the benefits of time management
- the qualities of a good time manager
- your personal time wasters and the consequences of wasting time
- solutions to common time wasting activities

## 12.2 The qualities of a good time manager

Imagine that you are a most effective time manager in an efficient office. Your colleagues admire you and want to model their work style on yours. What qualities would they list if they tried to write them out in order to copy them? The list might include:
-   effective delegation of tasks with trust and without micromanagement
-   respect for the time of others
-   positive thinking and decisiveness. (Sometimes the need is for a decision while the actual solution may be less important e.g. we do need to know immediately whether to drive on the left or the right hand side of the road but the actual decision does not actually matter!)
-   flexibility
-   problem solving ability
-   meeting deadlines and helping others to do the same Add your own ideas to this list.

## 12.3 Time wasters

This list is easier to compile because they are so common to so many.

### Habits
- postponing
- unnecessary long conversations unrelated to work
- inability to prioritise tasks
- just going slow
- not having objectives
- inability to cope with conflicting demands
- not delegating
- poor filing and organisation of papers: wasted time in searching for documents **People**
- informal meetings and trivial protracted greetings
- interruptions which disturb/delay an important discussion
- lack of puntuality
- pressures
- group therapy ("You will never believe what my partner wanted me to........!")
- duplicated effort
- confused communication leading to lack of cooperation and coordination
- confused lines of authority **Things**
- junk email and internet surfing
- playing computer/telephone games in work time
- mobile phones and changing settings
- transport
- badly designed space
- power cuts and no generator backup because of fuel lack from bad planning

Be honest with yourself. How many of these items are affecting you? Which of these are in your control and could be managed better? Are there others you could add?

> *"2) A Public Officer shall endeavour to accomplish planned activities on time. He or she shall desist from engaging in behaviour or conduct that disrupts or interferes with the work of other officers, such as, but not limited to:-*
> *a) Being lazy and idle at work.*
> *b) Reading newspapers most of the time, keeping the radio loud as to disrupt concentration, playing computer games or surfing the Internet*

All these lead to inefficiency, lack of a good outcome, hindrance to others, stress, and eventually loss of confidence. You have lowered morale, and lack time for yourself. Your reputation may suffer, opportunities and deadlines are lost, and productivity falls. You are definitely not succeeding in your work.

## 12.4 Time savers

In contrast there are some easily workable time savers and others for which you may need to advocate:
- organise your desk
- handle papers once: do it now then file immediately!
- make a job list with deadlines - in order of priority. If you have to do something which is not on your list, add it and give yourself the satisfaction of immediately crossing it out
- say "No" (nicely and diplomatically)
- give yourself reward breaks ("I will take tea only when this section is written")
- do a small task if you really cannot face a big one
- make sure your communications and management lines are clear and unambiguous
- improved technology but disciplined access to internet
- know your objectives and responsibilities
- plot a bar chart of your work in order to spread the load to become manageable

## 12.5 Procrastination

All of us have, on occasions, put off doing things which needed to be done. Here are some of the common reasons with ways to overcome them:

### Small versus large

We may busy ourselves with the small and easy tasks leaving the bigger ones until tomorrow. But tomorrow never comes! So start a big job, then reward yourself by doing an easy small one when you have reached a part-way goal. **Perfectionist**
We tell ourselves that we cannot do the job until we have all the information and the right conditions, and enough time. Perfection is the enemy of good. We must accept that a task is complete when we have done the best we can with the information at hand in the time available.

### The difficult phone call

We avoid speaking to the person about a difficult matter. Try phoning at lunch time and leaving a message with another person. **Waste of time**
We tell ourselves that there is no point in doing this task. If that is your belief you are not likely to do it well. See the person responsible and suggest an alternative. It is always better to tell your manager your suggested solution rather than your problem.

### Avoiding risky or new work

We make excuses to avoid working in an area of uncertainty. So break the task down into small bites. A journey around the world may seem terrifying but it starts with one small step.

## 12.6 Setting priorities

Your desk is littered with papers all of which need responses. You have shuffled through them several times and still do not know where to begin. In the past many office workers simply had an in-tray and an out-tray, but there are more effective ways of managing papers.

Start by organising your documents into three piles – URGENT, IMPORTANT, and SUPPORTIVE. If you have the luxury of a desk tray, these are your headings.

**URGENT:** there is a pressing deadline. Trouble will follow inactivity on this one. Others depend on it. It may not be critical but it will definitely not go away

**IMPORTANT:** work that keeps the wheels of the organisation turning. The deadline can be far away or not even exist. This may involve planning for a possible new building as expansion is inevitable

**SUPPORTIVE:** in this tray there will be professional journals, reports of meetings, documents that you want to read to be better informed.

Now decide what percentage of your time should be allocated to each tray given your job responsibilities. Perhaps 50 %, 40% and 10%? Is that how you are managing your time? If not, set realistic time percentages and adjust accordingly.

## 12.7 Managing your day

Fortunately we are not all at our best or worst at the same time. Some function well early in the morning: others late at night. Most of us have a dull period after the lunch break. We need to be clear when we are able to do tough work and when we are better at 'busy' work (flashy but not too important). Which is more appropriate for our mood? Make up your mind about the type of work you can and should do in a low energy period. You should also think about the high and low times of your colleagues as this may indicate when the best time is to meet with your manager!

You may find that you are doing work that is not your responsibility. Here is a quick test to make you aware of the need to delegate.

| QUESTION | YES | NO |
|---|---|---|
| 1. Do you take work home more than once a month? | | |
| 2. Do you work longer hours than the people you supervise? | | |
| 3. Are you frequently interrupted because others come to you for advice? | | |
| 4. Is some of your working time spent doing things for others that they could do for themselves? | | |
| 5. Do you have unfinished jobs accumulating with difficulty in meeting deadlines? | | |
| 6. Do you spend more time working on details than planning and supervising? | | |
| 7. Do you mistrust others to do the job as well as you might do it yourself? | | |
| 8. Do you work at details because you enjoy them, although someone else could do them? | | |
| 9. Do you doubt the abilities of your staff to take on more responsibilities? | | |
| 10. Are you a perfectionist, too conscientious about details that are not important for the main objectives of the job at hand? | | |
| 11. Do you keep job details secret from staff? | | |

| 12. Do you believe that you do your best work under pressure? | | |
| 13. Are you reluctant to admit that you need help to remain on top of your job? | | |
| 14. Do you fail to ask the team for their ideas about problems that arise at work? | | |
| 15. When you delegate tasks, do you try to micro-manage that person by checking the details of what has been done? | | |
| 16. Do you believe it is quicker to do it yourself? | | |

Nobody is perfect, but if you have replied "YES" more than six times, you should delegate more but without breaking confidentiality, of course. With more than 12 replies – plan for your heart attack. It may come sooner than you think.

The other side of delegating is that others may want to delegate tasks to you and you must avoid getting swamped or overloaded. Sometimes you just have to say "No". If this is your answer, then say it early, give a clear reason, or delegate other tasks, offer to review the situation at a later date, or propose another person.

## 12.8 Managing interruptions

Throughout the world, people enjoy greetings and these can be more protracted in some cultures than in others. "How are you? How is your day? How was your night? How was the weekend? How is your life? How is your wife?" It is good and proper to greet others, especially friends and colleagues. Sometimes a quick response is enough, "I'm fine". But when the greeting is an interruption of an important discussion with another, or sometimes it may come as an interruption of an interruption (!) then a significant conversation can be disrupted and time lost. Your boss pays you to deliver: you are not paid to chat endlessly in work time.

These days, perhaps the most common interruption is from a mobile phone. They ring during meetings, they ring from wrong numbers, and many just ring to chat. If you are talking to somebody, it is rude just to break off to answer a phone call. If a call is expected, warn the person at the start of your conversation. If it is not expected, quickly explain that you will call back. It is good discipline to turn phones off during a meeting. If the call is urgent, the caller will call back.

There are several techniques for avoiding time-wasting disturbances:
    e) Use your door as an indicator. Let your colleagues know that if it is closed you should not be disturbed. If it is open a little, you may be interrupted by something urgent/important. If it is wide open, come right in.
    f) Come to work a few minutes early for a quick round of your colleagues so that greetings are finished before your time to start work
    g) Arrange to go to lunch or tea breaks with others so that chatter can be shared in a relaxed period
    h) Set an example of not interrupting others
    i) If urgency demands an interruption, ask when it might be convenient to meet for an urgent matter
    j) Hold regular meetings for the exchange of work-related information
    k) You may have to say, "I'm sorry that I cannot talk now as we are discussing an important matter. May I suggest we go to lunch together?"

**12.9 Managing your desk** Simply:
- keep it tidy – deal with it – delegate it
- file it – don't just pile it!
- or bin it

*"2) A Public Officer shall, during official working hours, report his or her absence from office to his or her immediate supervisor or relevant persons. (The Code of Conduct for the Uganda Public Service, 2006)."*

Leave a note with contact phone number on your desk or door if you travel out of office so colleagues do not waste time trying to contact you.

**12.10 Summary tips**
- Be convinced that time management is worthwhile
- Just for one day, keep an honest diary of every 15 minutes of your time
- Analyse your time wasters and devise strategies to overcome them
- Plan your week
- Plan your day
- Write a job list
- Organise your in-tray (or desk piles) into URGENT, IMPORTANT and SUPPORTIVE
- Be aware of low and high times and tackle jobs appropriately
- Control interruptions
- Delegate more
- Be prepared to say "No"
- Share your ideas with your colleagues
- Plan what you will do with all your extra time now that you have changed into an efficient time manager!

# 11. How to Assess Your Personality

## 13.1 What are psychometric tests?

A psychometric test is a way of assessing a person's ability or personality in a measured and structured way. There are three main types of tests which examine ability, personality and interest. Some tests are used by employers to help them in their recruitment process while other tests can help people with career decision making.

It is common for graduate employers to use psychometric tests as part of their selection process. Organisations believe tests help them recruit the right people with the right mix of abilities and personal qualities. They are also useful for "sifting out" individuals from large numbers of applicants at an early stage and so saving the employers both time and money.

Tests can be administered by pen and paper or computer. You may be asked to take them in an assessment centre or online. If you take a psychometric test then as a candidate you should be provided with feedback. Do not trust an organisation that is not prepared to provide this. In the UK, because of the Data Protection Act, test providers have a legal responsibility to provide feedback if requested.

## 13.2 Types of test

## 1. Ability tests

- **General intelligence tests**
  Some tests assess your general ability (your intelligence). They are not dependent on prior learning or knowledge but more on how good you are at solving problems using logical thinking.
- **Specific ability tests**
  There are 2 types of specific ability tests:

### - Attainment tests

These examine the skills and knowledge you already possess. They are designed to assess what you know at the time of the test such as for a driving test or a word processing test. These can be known as work-related tests.

### - Aptitude tests

These are more of a measure of your potential for certain activities. They do not rely on any previous knowledge or training, but more on your natural ability or aptitude. The two most common forms of aptitude tests are verbal and numerical reasoning tests. There are also more specialised tests which can be used if you are applying for a particular career in IT, science or engineering.

## 2. Personality questionnaires

These are designed to allow organisations to measure aspects of your personality.  Unlike the tests listed above there are no right or wrong answers.  They seek to present a picture of how a person will behave in particular circumstances e.g. whether you are a 'leader' or a 'follower'. However, a personality assessment should always be followed by an interview with a qualified provider to validate the results of the assessment. This discussion with the user can explore relevant strengths and weaknesses for a job role or to assess their understanding of their behaviour.

## 3. Interest questionnaires

Interest inventories examine a person's interests and are often used in careers guidance. These can also be used for selection purposes.

## 13.3  Know yourself

Knowing your true self can come as a shock as we may not have the personality that we think we have. While many psychometric tests are available online there is a risk that we may simply not believe the results and consider a particular test as not applicable to everybody. But psychometric tests are based on the principles of being objective, valid and reliable. So testers may be more interested in your position on a scale than how high your mark is.

Some tests can only be applied by qualified and experienced psychologists. While many tests are available from the British Psychological Society, others will only be released to those who can establish their credentials (www.psychtesting.org.uk).

Other sites from which tests can be downloaded free include: www.doctorjob.com/testing zone, and www.shldirect.com which gives practical hints and tips as well as online practice. www.bradleycvs.co.uk offers a free test and a professional CV writing service. The Myers Briggs Personality Typing test has been used for many years and is most informative about yourself (www.personalitypathways.com). Emotions and Behaviours at Work is a newer site which is now being widely used internationally. You can trial it free and obtain an elaborate report through www.ebwonline.com.

# 12. How to Master Stress

## 14.1 Biology of stress

Our bodies have survival mechanisms for responding to immediate and long-term stress. However, one man's stress can be relaxation for another. While some are scared of spiders or walking along a cliff edge others actually enjoy the 'adrenaline rush' induced by bungee-jumping, mountaineering, extreme sports and free-falling from aeroplanes!

The immediate response to stress is dilatation of the eye pupils, an increase in heart and breathing rates, a rise in blood pressure and a shift in blood from the internal organs ('butterflies in the tummy') to the muscles of the arms and legs. Energy sources are mobilised into the blood stream from the liver. This has been called the "fright, flight or fight response". It is initiated by a special part of the nervous system and is reinforced for a longer period by adrenaline and other hormones released from the adrenal glands. In fact these physiological responses can be induced just by thinking about sitting in the dentist's chair! All this makes good physiological sense as the deer flees across the savannah ahead of a hungry lion; the mobilised energy compounds can be life saving in providing endurance.

However, if stress is not followed by exercise, then the mobilized energy chemicals can become dumped in the blood vessels later to form clots in the brain, heart or lungs and the blood pressure spikes can lead to organ damage.

Office workers and many others may experience many stresses - change of circumstances (sudden or extreme), lack of achievement through factors beyond their control, a sense of uncertainty and insecurity, linguistic isolation, deprivation, lack of family and friends, unfamiliar culture, high temperature, risk of tropical diseases, experience of conflict and life threatening situations.

## 14.2  Effects of stress

If stress becomes chronic and is not recognized or managed it can lead to several undesirable changes. These are mostly symptoms, not signs: they are feelings inside yourself and not necessarily obvious to others.

| BASIC STRESS | CUMULATIVE STRESS | TRAUMATIC STRESS |
|---|---|---|
| CONTROLLED | MANAGED | UNCONTROLLED |

They can include feelings of loneliness, emptiness, anger, hatred, frustration, swings in energy level and mood, concentration problems, restlessness, irritability, anxiety, fear, depression, sleep and digestive disturbances, re-experiencing events, self-reproach and guilt, even psychosomatic illness.

Sometimes pathological stress responses are not experienced until after your contract or posting to another region. Some organisations are giving more focus to the importance of self-awareness and care for colleagues who may be unaware that they are approaching burnout or total collapse. The United Nations has produced a thorough cover of the subject for staff and trainers (Managing the Stress of Humanitarian Emergencies, Geneva, July 2001); the older version (1995) includes a simple self-test which allows alert to early stress signals.

## 14.3   Techniques for coping with stress

Stress must be avoided or managed. Care can be taken before, during or after working in a new post or different location.

<u>Before</u>
- ask your family and friends to keep in touch to keep a sense of belonging and stability
- research well the situation to which you are going to prepare your mind for the changes and avoid surprises or shocks
- obtain a security briefing from the organisation (or your High Commission if going abroad or to a dangerous location
- take family/friends/personal photographs for display in your room and for sharing with new friends

<u>On Arrival</u>
- obtain an updated security briefing
- plan two mission statements (see Section 6)
- plan for leisure time and exercise
- keep contact with your home base
- start a journal in which you express your feelings. This can serve as a letter to family and is most cathartic in the process

<u>During</u>
- maintain your exercise and leisure schedule
- stay aware of stress signals in yourself and colleagues
- remind yourself that the contract is not for ever
- discipline yourself to say "No" to further requests for help/work
- learn meditation (especially easy if you are in Asia. Try a Vipassena 11-day silent meditation programme at a Goenke Ashram which can give you valuable life-long mental tools)
- network socially with compatriots
- develop muscle relaxation techniques. These can be useful sleep inducers or used during sleepless nights without having to resort to hypnotic medicines. A stressed mind causes tense muscles (ready for Flight or Fight). If you can relax the muscles, you can also relax the mind.

Here are four well-tested methods:
1. Experience a good massage from a professional. But be selective as many massage parlours have other intentions. (Disabuse your mind of the idea that a sauna is relaxing - physiologically it is highly stressful).
2. Lie on your back and rest your hands on stomach or thighs. Now work through your body, starting with your feet and progressing to your face: tense the muscles. Hold the position - and relax. Bend your feet towards your knees hard; hold them in tension for a few seconds. Then relax. Repeat for your calves, thighs, buttocks,

back, abdomen, chest and arms, neck and face (in a silent scream). Make sure the relaxation is complete and check from time to time that muscle blocks stay limp after tension. There are good tape recordings of music and instruction available if a prompt is needed.

3. A more advanced approach is to leave out the tension components and use your mind alone to ensure relaxation using the same progression from feet to head. This can be combined with observing the sensations in your skin where it contacts with the bed, and registering the sensations in your mind with detachment and equanimity. Just be aware, and survey the whole surface of your body systematically. Do you feel itch? Tingling? Pressure? Discomfort? With practice you can extend the approach to leaving the skin and entering body cavities such as the ears and mouth.

4. Slow breathing has been demonstrated to lower blood pressure, slow the heart rate and induce relaxation. We usually use two sets of muscles for breathing: the diaphragm and those between the ribs. While you are reading this, place your left hand on the bottom of your rib cage under your right arm. Try breathing only with your diaphragm when no movement will be felt here. Now take a huge breath in as if in panic; your rib cage will move up and out as in excessive exercise.

   While lying on your back you are going to change your breathing from about 12 times a minute to half that amount. Concentrating on diaphragmatic breathing, Inhale maximally for six counts (seconds), hold for three, exhale totally with a deep sigh for six to nine, and hold for three; repeating the controlled breaths. Do this ten times for a start and increase to slow breathing for 15 minutes later if you can.

The last three exercises are best done lying on your back in bed but they can be practiced anywhere and at any time, even sitting at your computer or standing waiting for a bus.

On returning home do seek help or counselling if you need it. There is no shame associated with returning home wounded after a tough assignment

# 13. How to Pursue Distance Learning Courses

**15.1 Who is distance learning for?**
This section is a Study Guide for people who want to put their experience and knowledge in a wider context by studying a course through 'distance learning' methods and it is suitable for those who need an introduction to the subject. Such students will be helped if they can also attend a short full time course in a related area to provide the added advantage of sharing experiences with others. Distance learning is usually based on a combination of reading materials, assignments and sometimes field or practical work under the guidance of a tutor. The programme may be supported by audio-visual material, computer links and virtual class mates through internet. These may form a group for mutual support and encouragement, and may be spread over wide areas yet never actually meet.

## Aims

This guide aims to provide
- an introduction to distance learning
- an indication of the advantages and problems associated with distance learning • suggested study techniques for overcoming the problems

## How long will each module take?

Distance learning (sometimes called 'open learning') modules may form complete courses or be components of a larger programme. The time taken will depend on the level and the ability of the learner and previous experience. This Study Guide will take about one hour of work.

## Advantages of open learning

Open learning gives you the choices to study when, where, and for as long as you wish. You also have freedom to concentrate on those areas that are more interesting to you or that are more relevant to your work. However, you will need self-discipline and may still need support from others.

## Can I cope with distant learning?

Universities and colleges in many countries offer distance learning programmes of study. Of the 70 universities in the UK, the Open University is the largest with over 200,000 students worldwide. That is only one of many universities and other organisations established globally which use distance learning methods. Thousands of other ordinary people progress by this means - so can you. Nevertheless, you will have to take more control of your learning than you did when you were in a more traditional learning situation such as at school. These modules are intended to be *worked through,* and not just *read;* this study guide will help you to do this successfully.

**15.2 What learning techniques will I be using?** Distance
Learning programmes may include:

- pre- and post-module tests
- frequent tasks and activities
- 'stop and think' breaks
- fieldwork to be done away from your desk or work place
- interviews and fact-finding exercises
- broader questions and topics to think about and discuss
- case studies drawn from a range of countries
- suggestions for group discussions with friends and colleagues
- suggestions for further reading and study

**15.3 How can I plan my study?**

To get the most out of your course you need to plan your approach to study. Many people also benefit from encouragement to keep going. So select a 'study-buddy' (a teaching helper or mentor) with whom you can talk about the course and who will undertake to check your progress from time to time. The study-buddy could be another student of the same course, or may be a colleague or friend who has an interest in the subject, but need not necessarily be a person experienced in the subject. A learning helper will provide the opportunity for meaningful and stimulating discussion. This is most important for the testing, expansion, and reinforcement of the ideas and concepts that you will gain from the course. Once you have chosen a study-buddy, you need to negotiate with that person what his or her role will be. The study-buddy could:

- check your progress regularly
- comment on your written work
- discuss suggested topics with you
- give you advice about field work locations
- provide encouragement

*Do I need personal objectives?*

Yes, you do. You will need to think about why you are taking the course and what you hope to gain from it. You may need something to do at the weekends, or you hope to be better at your job. You may want to see if you have the ability to cope with a more advance course of study by distance learning. Or perhaps you just want a break from the pressures of your employment. Any of these is a valid reason for study and you may have other ideas.

*Self-study* is more demanding than traditional classroom instruction because you will need to provide your own framework for study instead of having it imposed on you by the course or workshop timetable. You will have to be self-motivated and disciplined enough to continue when a 'voice inside' is telling you to stop. One of the problems of self-study is that some people begin with great enthusiasm at a pace that cannot be sustained. The best way to start a self-study course is to plan your own study schedule over a pre-set period by thinking ahead and making your own timetable.

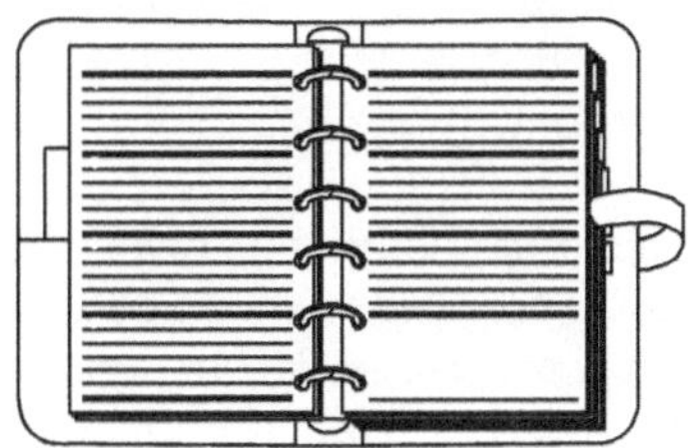

Your **timetable** will specify the days and the hours that you have set aside for study each week. Ideally, these arrangements will be agreed with your study-buddy who can support you in this resolve. So write the scheduled time in your diary or on a chart displayed over your working area. You may be able to get the agreement of your boss or colleagues to allow some of the study time (on a regular and undisturbed basis, of course!) to be included within working hours. Organise your work area to allow this.

**Schedule** your timing around events, such as holidays or travel or high-stress employment times.

Here are other methods to help your learning:
1.  Develop a study reflex by studying consistently in a place, which you associate with work. Do not try to study when lying on your bed.

This location is associated with sex, or sleep – and that is what will happen!

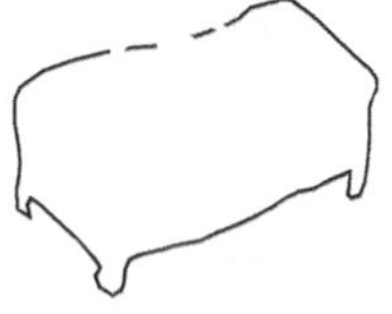

You will study best if you always study in the same chair in the same place with a good light. This will help you develop a 'study reflex'. If your concentration starts to fail then move to another place and relax. Keep that study place for concentrated work, not for other trivial activities such as eating and relaxing. If you have only one place, then simply make another by turning your chair through 180 degrees, or placing it at the side of the same desk or table.

2. Reward yourself with short breaks of physical or different activities or cups of tea *after* you have completed a particular task or studied for a predetermined period of time (e.g. one hour).

ɔ

3. Discourage 'study busters' among your friends and family by putting a notice on the door saying, "GONE AWAY". You may also hang a line of dirty underclothes, socks and other washing across the inside of the door to discourage those who are really determined to disturb your concentration!

The most demanding study busters are children. Especially your own. It is difficult to explain to a three-year old child who is appealing for attention that Mum or Dad must not be disturbed "because they are engaged in cerebral activities associated with an important distance learning programme of international significance concerning emergency management"! Unusually supportive collaboration between partners is needed to cope with this situation.

4. Travelling and waiting time can be used for revision. Prepare notes in small writing on pocket-sized cards or pieces of paper (one quarter the size of this page) which can be carried easily in pockets or bags, and refer to them while waiting for bus, train or ox/camel cart.

5. Use *active* learning techniques. This means asking yourself questions that you or your study-buddy would like answered *before* you read the material. Then search for the answers in the material provided. At the end, review the main points *and explore their use in your work*. Only when knowledge is applied does it becomes a skill.

*"I hear, and I forget.*
*I see, and I remember.*
*I do, and I understand."*

**15.4 What do I do if I get behind with my work?**

Unexpected events may occur to delay your progress. Don't panic! This is a common experience.

1. Read the regulations that govern your course again. There may be allowances for some assignments to be skipped or delayed
2. Check that you have set yourself realistic goals and adjust them if necessary
3. Inform your tutor and ask for guidance rather than inventing excuses
4. Seek support or suggestions from your study-buddy or a fellow student

5. Remember that 'perfection' means doing the best that you can in the time available. It does not mean putting into your assignment, every single example and reference. Be selective. In the last resort you may need to complete some tasks at a lower standard then you normally set for yourself to help you catch up.
*Perfection is the enemy of good!*

*A last piece of advice before you start another module.*

## THE SQ3R READING METHOD

Any distance learning and self-study programme will involve a large amount of reading. Perhaps you have already had the experience of reading a page of a book, or a whole chapter, after which you realise that none of the information has been registered or remembered. Indeed, it is possible to read even a short paragraph mechanically while your mind is far from the subject. This can easily apply if you are feeling tired, or you have had a stressful day at work.

The SQ3R (**s**urvey, **q**uestion, **r**ead, **r**ecall, **r**eview) reading method is well tried, world-wide, and it can also help you to overcome concentration and memory problems with reading.

### Survey

Before studying a book, a chapter, or any written material, survey the whole piece of writing by scanning it quickly to get an outline of its content. Key information is often contained in the introductory or concluding (summary) paragraphs. Important information is often to be found in the first sentence of a paragraph, while the rest may be an expansion or development of the same idea. Look at the table of contents, glance at the tables and figures, and note especially lists of important points. This will tell you if you should spend more time reading the material carefully.

### Question

Your reading will lead to active learning and be more easily remembered if you formulate a few specific questions for which you are searching for answers. If there are headings in the material, turn the heading into a question. E.g. If the heading is "Impediments to Returning", change the heading (in your head) to "What are the Impediments to Returning?" But ask yourself other questions as well.

### Read

Read at whatever speed is comfortable for you. At the same time make notes about the information in your own words, or use a highlighter pen to indicate important ideas. (However, you should not make marks in a book or journal which has been lent to you by a friend, or borrowed from a library!)

### Recall

Now close the book or other volume, and work hard to recall what you have read, section by section. This is more valuable than rereading because it forces you to actively remember. You are not expected to recite the text word for word, but to see whether you have picked up the main ideas and facts. For maximum learning, the recall should take place *as soon as possible* after the reading. The longer you leave it, the more information will be forgotten. If you do not try to recall, you may just fool yourself into thinking that you have done some serious work.

**Review**

Finally, review what you have written and read. Again, this is most effective if done soon after the initial study. It is far better to do this than leaving the review to a 'swotting period' just before a test or examination, and perhaps long after your initial study.

> **Reinforcement of your knowledge.** Ask any teachers or lecturers when they best learned their subject – when they were students, or when they taught the subject. All will say that mastery of a subject is best acquired by teaching it to others. So teachers are the best students and you will

have to become a teacher if you are to become confident  about your knowledge in your new field of study. This

> module, therefore, will conclude with a small teaching

exercise. Be prepared for it!

> **Take every opportunity to teach others about the things you are learning.**

### STOP AND THINK.

• *Then write down the answers to the following 8 questions:*

1. What are your personal reasons for studying this course?

2. Who would you like as your study-buddy?

3. What would you like your study-buddy to do?

4. What will you do for your study-buddy in return for the help?

5. To what extent will your partner/friends support your studies? Ask them to protect your study time.

6. Plan your study times and write them in your diary, or make a chart. How many weeks have you planned for each module?

7. Where have you decided to study?

8. Have I asked my boss if I can study at work?

*ACTIVITY*

*Explain to your study-buddy the advantages and disadvantages of distance learning. What techniques can you use to overcome the difficulties? Then teach your study helper about the use and value of the SQ3R reading method without referring to this document. Give your helper a relevant article and test the method together.*

FOR THOSE WHO ARE BEGINNERS IN THE FIELD OF HUMANITARIAN WORK YOU MAY LIKE TO OBTAIN A FREE DISTANCE LEARNING MODULE CALLED "REFUGEES AND INTERNALLY DISPLACED PERSONS (IDPs). Download it from www.distancelearning.org.

This module will allow you to explore distance learning without any outside commitment. It is self assessed and covers an introduction to disaster terminology, the global disaster situation, the differences between refugees and IDPs, the Sphere Minimum Standards, the Deng Humanitarian Guiding Principles, and a case study from Sri Lanka.

**YOU ARE NOT ALONE IN CYBERSPACE!**

Distance learning can be lonely but it need not be. Access to internet and e-mail facilities gives you access to information and also to people. People like yourself who are following the same programme. There are people 'out there' with whom you can share ideas and mutual support.

**Use Internet to:**

Obtain documents. The world library is available from your keyboard.

Create virtual classrooms with class mates. You can keep in touch by e-mail, listserve (regular topics for those interested in the same subjects), newsgroups, and live chats through programmes like Yahoo Messenger and Skype. The latter is truly fantastic. It can be downloaded free and if you have internet facilities you can talk free of charge to anywhere in the world providing your correspondent has obtained the same facilities. With a cheap headset you will think your Skype partner is in the same room as yourself. You can also use Skype to phone other non-Skype users for almost nothing.

## 14. How to Work as a Manager – answer these questions

1. What management style and characteristics do I most value in my line manager?
2. What are the characteristics of my management style?
   Autocratic/democratic/creative/consultative/decisive/flexible/predictable/bureaucratic?
   Do I delegate with trust?
3. Do I hold regular staff meetings to inform and to be informed?
4. Do I know how to stimulate/motivate staff, get them to set goals and monitor their progress? Do I know how to audit their activities, measure successes and failures, provide appropriate action (encouragement, remedial activities)? How do I build the team?
5. Are there adequate opportunities for ALL issues in the group to be discussed in a nonjudgemental manner?
6. Am I punctual with all my activities (deadlines)?
7. Are meetings held on time? Are they managed well?
8. Are agendas available before the meetings?
9. Are minutes produced and shared with all parties immediately after meetings?
10. Are new staff given a warm welcome? Are office systems explained?
11. Are appropriate briefings given to all visitors to the office?
12. Do I develop respect among colleagues by my example?
13. Would the team follow me into 'battle'?
14. Am I aware of the team spirit and atmosphere? Do I know when some have problems? Do I check if apparent negative views are shared by others? Do I really care?
15. Do I consult with others *in their offices* on a regular and friendly basis? Is my office door open for them?
16. Do I take up too much of their time by talking too much when they are trying to work?
17. When I talk to them do I check out that they want to hear what I am saying? Do I read their body language if they are trying to get away?
18. Are my written and oral messages clear and unambiguous? Are they confusing?
19. Do I really believe that the programme is the most important aspect of the work, and that staff should be helped, not hindered by bureaucratic procedures? Am I committed to the idea that administrative staff should work efficiently to support and encourage the work of Programme/Field staff?
20. Have I analysed my inadequacies and ensured that they are compensated by team members or my own remedial activities? Do I try to appoint those who are more able than me?
21. Do I think that management skill is inborn, or am I committed to the view that I need to update regularly (by reading/workshop/course) my management skills?
22. Do I allow staff to feed back to me (after giving adequate notice) how they feel about my management style?

23. How do staff rate me as a manager? How does my boss rate me as a manager? How do I rate myself as a manager? What can I do to explain or rectify mismatches?
24. How do I deal with conflict between colleagues, or between colleagues and myself?
25. Do I make available to staff a 'folder' with documentation of all administrative procedures so that staff can find out for themselves how systems work?
26. Is the office documentation well organised and easily available to staff? Are staff encouraged to use literature and improve their knowledge?
27. What am I doing to help staff to reach their potential?
28. Do I help staff to keep refreshed and updated on use of English in reports and presentations, bureaucratic procedures, transport, security, welfare and emergency procedures?
29. Do I send staff on courses and conferences and encourage their networking with other agencies and humanitarian workers?
30. Do I give balanced attention to the office buildings, materials/equipment, staff and processes?

## 15. How to Help a New Colleague

A new colleague arrives in your Department. To assist that person to become a productive member of the team as soon as possible has obvious benefit. If new colleagues are left to find their own way they may have feelings of insecurity and make mistakes. A better way is for the line manager to appoint an experienced peer to act as a mentor initially and for as long as necessary, or for a period of time agreed between the two people.

On the day your new team member arrives, with some preparation, only two or three hours are needed for the following programme.

Start by checking that satisfactory accommodation has been obtained. Then give:

1. An introduction to the site and where to go for domestic facilities (toilets, refreshments, and emergency health care)
2. Background information about transport, banks and other facilities in the locality
3. An introduction to colleagues
4. Background to the District
5. Building arrangements and office space - chair, desk, electricity for computer if needed, filing cabinet or storage space, (or description of current and future building plans)
6. Security arrangements: security guards, room cleaning and locking/unlocking of doors
7. Discussion about the structure of the organisation and systems
8. Terms of reference - salary, leave, sick leave, expenses/claims for travel
9. A letter of appointment
10. Schedule of meetings to be attended
11. Detailed discussion of Work Plan proposals, ways to be of use, and immediate activities in your group
12. A map of the area and travel methods for field work (if applicable). Census data may also be appropriate
13. Guidance on procedure for contacting outside organisations
14. Information about administrative matters
    a. Daily signing in arrangements

b.  Obtaining stationary
c.  Administrative assistance with typing, procuring etc
d.  Photocopying
e.  Computing facilities
f.  Printing documents
g.  Internet facilities

15. General discussion on protocols (dress, address for politicians)
16. Arrangements for weekly meetings for awareness of events and activities
17. Access to relevant files and their locations - Annual Work Plan, Financial Year, others?
18. A staff list of key personnel and contact numbers

# 16. <u>How to Decide Whether to Change Jobs</u>

## 16.1 Why Think About a Change

Any of several factors might make you think about changing your present employment for another:
- A seemingly less able colleague has moved on or been promoted
- You feel you are stagnating
- Domestic responsibilities are demanding more income
- You have difficult work mates or an overbearing manager
- Raised delivery targets are causing too much stress
- The present work has become boring
- You need easier travelling in order to have more time to care for      relatives, or to spend with your family
- You have not been promoted nor had a salary rise for too long -   Nobody seems to appreciate the contributions you have made to      the organisation
- You would just like a change

Before changing employment several aspects should be carefully explored:

1.      What does my manager or the organisation really think of me? If superiors knew I was looking elsewhere, would I be encouraged to go or to stay? How can I find out?

2.      What other opportunities are available within or outside my organisation that I could match? I need to look in newspapers and other places where adverts are placed e.g. notice boards and magazines. First I should look at other possible positions in my company. Importantly I must also network with my contacts to find potential opportunities

3.    I have not been interviewed since the selection for my present post and interview experience would be valuable before applying for the perfect job. Perhaps applying for any possible opening would update my interview experience

4.    Can I do anything to enhance my current promotion or other employment prospects? Should I be taking some further studies, obtain further qualifications or attend more workshops to widen my experience? Should I ask my manager to give me more responsibilities?

Other important considerations include:
- Salary. Money is needed for survival. I should think of a 10% increase but I could move sideways if other factors compensated or if a guaranteed rise was imminent
- Other financial inducements could compensate for a move with little salary increase. These could be costs provided for: children's education, health care expenses, travel, food, car allowance, pension contribution, insurance cover, office equipment, printing business cards, computer/printer availability, photocopying, telephone calls, pens and stationary, loans or advances
- Travel time and therefore costs
- Working hours and number of leave days
- Job satisfaction and stress level: targets and expectations of delivery
- Educational opportunities: courses, workshops, study expenses, study time allowance
- Working environment: space, office furniture, privacy, facilities (food, bank, access to shops in lunch time), colleagues
- Potential for increased responsibilities (staff, facilities, finance management, promotion and/or salary increments)

## 16.2 How to Think About Change

Before considering possible job opportunities write down what you like in your present job and what you do not like. Writing down clarifies the mind so you can focus on possible assets of a potential new position. For example –

| I LIKE | I DO NOT LIKE |
| --- | --- |
| My colleagues | Bureaucratic illogical procedures |
| Having flexible hours | Financial accounting |
| Always having free weekends | Too many deadlines |
| Support for short courses | The company ethics |
| Managing people | The office conditions |
| Taking leave days whenever I like | A long journey to work |
| Recognition for my work | External noise and pollution |
| Etc | Etc |

Think carefully about these items because they can tell you something about yourself. Your friendly colleagues are important; you listed those first. Perhaps you work better as a team member than alone. You do not like bureaucracy. You prefer freedom to work in your own way: you may be better as a teacher than as a civil servant. Now you know what to look for in a new opportunity. You may also have highlighted that if you had some training in accounting methods, financial management might not be so distasteful.

## 16.3 Planning the Change

Once you have identified a new possibility you need to make comparisons between it and your present position and there are several ways of doing this. A large salary increase may be the only inducement you need; you will put up with the rest! Or you may wish to evaluate the two posts in a fuller comparative way to avoid jumping out of the frying pan into the fire. So another approach is to tabulate, according to a range of criteria, aspects which you consider important in your work. The following table lists some examples. Some may not be relevant to your interests; there may be others that you would add and which are particularly significant in your own circumstances e.g. your journey to work is long but it takes you passed the factory where your wife is employed so she can be dropped off each morning and collected in the evening. You will think of other criteria.

It is difficult to quantify many of the factors you have listed. While a 'salary' can be measured precisely, 'friendly colleagues' cannot. So use a star rating system (or a 1 to 5 scale of rating) for each category. While different categories will differ in importance, you will see a pattern emerging that will help you to reach a decision. Importantly, discuss the overall picture with your partner, family, trustworthy colleagues and friends. Comments can be added to clarify the items under consideration. Put a question mark if unsure and this will suggest questions to be asked at an interview. Try completing the table for your current work.

<table>
<tr><td colspan="4" align="center">EMPLOYMENT EVALUATION</td></tr>
<tr><td>CONSIDERATIONS</td><td>Present Post</td><td>Proposed Post</td><td>COMMENTS</td></tr>
<tr><td>GENERAL CONDITIONS</td><td></td><td></td><td></td></tr>
<tr><td>Salary</td><td>***</td><td>*****</td><td>Take-home pay after tax and other stoppages</td></tr>
<tr><td>Working hours</td><td>*</td><td>**</td><td>Include work at home and travel time</td></tr>
<tr><td>Leave days</td><td>**</td><td>****</td><td>How soon can you take leave after starting?</td></tr>
<tr><td>Other financial inducements</td><td>***</td><td>?</td><td>Per diem and lunch allowance</td></tr>
<tr><td>Pension</td><td>0</td><td>*****</td><td>Does the organisation contribute to a pension?</td></tr>
<tr><td>Health care</td><td>***</td><td>?</td><td>Who will pay for health care and sick leave?</td></tr>
<tr><td>Administrative support</td><td>**</td><td>*****</td><td>Etc</td></tr>
<tr><td>Job satisfaction</td><td>*</td><td>****</td><td>Etc</td></tr>
<tr><td>Stress level</td><td>*****</td><td>*</td><td></td></tr>
<tr><td>Current staff turnover</td><td>*</td><td>*****</td><td></td></tr>
<tr><td>Stability of the organisation</td><td>*</td><td>*****</td><td></td></tr>
<tr><td>DOMESTIC IMPACT</td><td></td><td></td><td></td></tr>
<tr><td>Time with family and friends</td><td></td><td></td><td></td></tr>
<tr><td>My travel time</td><td></td><td></td><td></td></tr>
<tr><td>Overall income</td><td></td><td></td><td></td></tr>
<tr><td>Use of transport (motorcycle, car)</td><td></td><td></td><td></td></tr>
<tr><td>SOCIAL FACTORS</td><td></td><td></td><td></td></tr>
<tr><td>Work environment</td><td></td><td></td><td></td></tr>
<tr><td>Friendly colleagues</td><td></td><td></td><td></td></tr>
<tr><td>Access to amenities</td><td></td><td></td><td></td></tr>
<tr><td>Need to relocate accommodation</td><td></td><td></td><td></td></tr>
<tr><td>Ethically sound (not corrupt)</td><td></td><td></td><td></td></tr>
<tr><td>Insurance cover</td><td></td><td></td><td></td></tr>
<tr><td>Achievement of my potential</td><td></td><td></td><td></td></tr>
<tr><td>Contribution to society</td><td></td><td></td><td></td></tr>
<tr><td>FUTURE WORK POTENTIAL</td><td></td><td></td><td></td></tr>
<tr><td>Increased responsibilities generally</td><td></td><td></td><td></td></tr>
<tr><td>Increased management of people</td><td></td><td></td><td></td></tr>
<tr><td>Increased management of finances</td><td></td><td></td><td></td></tr>
<tr><td>Increased management of things</td><td></td><td></td><td></td></tr>
<tr><td>Increased work load overall</td><td></td><td></td><td></td></tr>
<tr><td>Attendance on courses and workshops</td><td></td><td></td><td></td></tr>
<tr><td>Paid study leave</td><td></td><td></td><td></td></tr>
<tr><td>Retirement age</td><td></td><td></td><td></td></tr>
</table>

Remember that a tough job with a supportive work team and family can be totally satisfying. In contrast, the finest job in the world can be made miserable by one horrible colleague.

The author has found, in a varied life, that if a year passes and you have added nothing to your *curriculum vitae*, it is probably time to move. Once you have made the decision to stay put, or change, stick with it. "Feel the Fear and do it Anyway" (as one author titled his book), because you may never know whether your decision was right or wrong.